Learning the Secrets of Solitude and Silence

(Creating Those Moments That Bring Healing and Renewal to Our Mind, Body, and Spirit)

By Denise George

In the Quiet Place we learn to seek, drink in, and treasure our silent times alone with God.

**Learning the Secrets of Solitude and Silence
by Denise George**
All rights reserved.
Copyright 2011

This book or parts thereof may not be reproduced in any form, stored in a retrieval system, or transmitted in any form by any means without prior written permission of the author, except as provided by United States of America copyright law.

Previously published by Bethany House Publishers as *Come to the Quiet.*

Cover design: Hyliian Graphics, Elizabeth E. Little, http://hyliian.deviantart.com
Interior design: Ellen C. Maze www.ellencmaze.com
Published by: *Sine Qua Non* Publications

ISBN-13: 978-1468031362

Also available in eBook publication

Author Website: www.authordenisegeorge.com

All scripture was utilized from the New International Version (NIV) Bible translations unless otherwise noted in the text.

PRINTED IN THE UNITED STATES OF AMERICA

Dedication:

For Carolyn Tomlin and Matt Tomlin,
my special friends.

"Then, because so many people were coming and going that they did not even have a chance to eat, [Jesus] said to them, *Come with Me by yourselves to a Quiet Place and get some rest*. So they went away by themselves in a boat to a solitary place."
~ Mark 6:31-32 NIV

A Word to You, My Reader:

I meet women every day—in every walk of life, in every age group, with children and without children, who work inside and/or outside the home—who are mentally exhausted, physically depleted, and emotionally/spiritually drained.

No doubt, you meet them too. You may, in fact, be one of them. If so, I have written this book especially for you.

Exhaustion has become the new look of the twenty-first century women! Not long ago, I interviewed hundreds of Christian women for my new book with Zondervan titled: *What Women Wish Pastors Knew*. Almost each woman told me her number one issue in life was *exhaustion*. "Please Denise," they said in unison, "Please tell our pastors we're tired!"

As you already know, our present society is restless. We can look into the average woman's eyes and see her weariness. The eyes can't conceal exhaustion. We can look into a mirror and see our own weariness. Women today generally have too many responsibilities to manage, too many jobs to handle, and too many demands on our already over-worked bodies. Stress, worry, guilt, and society's anxieties can play havoc with our emotions.

Let me ask you a few questions. When was the last time you stopped on a warm summer morning and breathed in the fragrance of freshly mowed grass? When was the last time you sat down just to listen to spring's raindrops tap against your window? How long has it been since you had a quiet moment to refresh yourself with a cup of herbal tea or other refreshing drink? Or shared a dinner with a friend "just for fun?" Or read a book of fiction from cover to cover in one sitting? Or fished on the bank of a river on a peaceful afternoon?

Can't remember? Then read this book carefully, and listen to the One who loves you and who calls you to come to Him for healing, solitude, and silent communion.

The Question: In response to my question, most women honestly answer, "It's been a long time since I've stopped and rested." For many women, "rest" is that unexpected and unscheduled white space on their daily calendars. They allow themselves to rest only when they've not planned something else to do, or when no one else has planned something for them to do. How often the unexpressed (and expressed) expectations of others keep us constantly busy!

Within these pages, I want to introduce you to something more powerful than just a nap in the middle of the day, or an hour to sit and rest weary muscles. I want to introduce you to soul-satisfying, deeply spiritual, peaceful, renewing communion spent in the Quiet Place with the One who loves, heals, and comforts His daughters.

Most women I meet suffer with exhausted minds, minds that must constantly keep up with complicated schedules, minds that are stretched to their limits with increasing demands and responsibilities. They also suffer with tired bodies, bodies that work far too hard and run in too many different directions. And they suffer with weary souls, souls that are weighed down with stress and pain and worry and guilt. Spirits whose vessels have run dry and need to be filled up to the brim with fresh Living Water. (1)

I know of few women these days that make regular scheduled time to treasure quiet solitude with God. Some complain: "I don't have time." Others tell me: "I have too many people depending on me, and too many responsibilities."

Over the years I have discovered that if a woman doesn't make time to spend with God in quiet solitude, she will soon register "empty" in body, mind, emotions, and spirit. Maybe you have already registered "empty." Just as our car requires gasoline and regular maintenance to run, we also need spiritual fuel and silence and solitude. God has called us to a journey of loving, helping, and ministering to others in his name. If we don't incorporate quiet time with him into our travels, we will end up wrecked somewhere along life's roadside. We will join the other tired and empty women who were unable to continue their journeys. Throughout the ages women have driven themselves into "dis-ease" and even death simply because they overworked and overstressed their bodies, minds, and spirits.

I invite you to join me throughout the pages of this book, and learn how to experience the hope and peace that God will bring you through solitude and quiet. While you read, ask God to direct you, transform you, and bring you closer to his image. Come to the Quiet Place where Jesus waits, learn the secrets of healing and renewal, and allow God to work a transforming miracle in your mind, body, and spirit.

Hurting Women: I have been writing books to help "hurting women" for many years. God has laid this particular ministry on my heart. He has opened the doors for me to write, publish, and reach out to thousands of women who urgently need to know his love and care.

My prayer is that you, or whomever you give the gift of this book, might find comfort, peace, and assurance in these words, and know, without a doubt, how very much God loves and cares for you. Nothing in life is more important than your intimate and trusting relationship with the Lord.

If this book helps you, please email me and let me know. My email address is: cdwg@aol.com. My website address is: www.authordenisegeorge.com. You can find other books in this series on my blog:
http://encouragementforwoundedwomen.blogspot.com.

May God richly bless you and keep you.

(This book is available as both an ebook to download and a printed book to order. You can order it online at my website.)

~ Denise George

Come to Me, all you who labor and are heavy laden, and I will give you rest.
~ Matthew 11:28 NKJV

Table of Contents

Section One: Healing the Mind .... - 1 -
Chapter 1: Mama's Shoulder 1
Chapter 2: Our Mind—Created for Quiet 5
Chapter 3: Mind Attack! 10
Chapter 4: Resting Our Mind in Christ 15
Chapter 5: Letting Christ Transform Our Mind 21
Section Two: Healing the Body 25
Chapter 6: Today's Woman—Overworked! 26
Chapter 7: Stress Attack! 36
Chapter 8: Job Stress 42
Chapter 9: Majoring in the Minors 47
Chapter 10: De-Stressing and Resting Our Body 57
Chapter 11: Transforming Our Body 62
Section Three: Healing the Spirit 65
Chapter 12: Yoked with Heavy Burdens 66
Chapter 13: Guarding Our Heart to Actively Love 70
Chapter 14: Finding Nurture and Nourishment 76
Chapter 15: The Transformation of Our Soul 83
About the Author 88
Also by Denise George 90
Endnotes 96

Section 1

Healing
the Mind

Jesus said: "Come to Me…"
~ Matthew 11:28 NKJV

Chapter 1

Mama's Shoulder

> "The person who wants to arrive at interiority and spirituality has to leave the crowd behind and spend some time with Jesus.... Cultivate the solitude of your cell, and guard against the invasions of your quietude."
> ~ Thomas a Kempis (2)

The year was 1956. I was five years old. My mother, grandmother, and I had been shopping, and I was exhausted. We had been in and out of all the busy stores that lined the length of fashionable Rossville Boulevard on that cool Saturday afternoon in northern Georgia. My young mind whirled with all the frantic activity that surrounded us. We still had two more places to shop: Loveman's Department Store and Bon-Ton's Dress Shop. I was worn out, but my mother's shopping energy got a new burst when she saw the 75-percent-discount sale sign in Bon-Ton's window. That's when my wise grandmother, "Mama," noticed my limp arms and legs and glazed-over eyes. She diagnosed correctly that I had a bad case of "shopper's shock." She took me by the hand, and said, "Come with me, 'Nisey," and led me away from the chaotic crowd.

Willene," she called to my mother above the noise and din of shoppers. "You go into Bon-Ton's. 'Nisey and I will wait for you in the car."

I shall forever thank Mama for that brilliant suggestion! Looking back more than a half-century later, I now realize that

Learning the Secrets of Solitude and Silence

Mama was also tired! We forced our way against the flow of bargain-hunters and escaped through the maze to my mother's large black Chevrolet. Once inside the comfortable interior, I breathed a sigh of relief. I had finally found a quiet place, a place of solitude with my beloved grandmother, far from the hustle and bustle of salespeople and shoppers.

Tired and Sleepy: I laid my head on my grandmother's shoulder as we settled into the car's front seat. I felt her soft woolen coat against my face. I smelled the lingering vanilla flavoring she had spooned into that morning's fresh-baked pound cakes. I closed my eyes and listened to her breathing. I heard her reassuring words gently urging me, "Be still, 'Nisey, and rest."

A storm of sorts brewed outside our car: a shower of shoppers; to my small ears, thunderous traffic and lightning bolts of sharp words shouted over the downtown street's few parking spaces. Inside, however, Mama's shoulder provided a secure sanctuary of peace, tranquility, and safety from the storm.

I opened my eyes to disrupt my rest only once. From the car window, I saw people hurrying in and out of the stores, lugging packages and bags. I watched white-gloved mothers tug at tired little girls who had sore feet stuffed into new patent leather shoes. I saw old women wearing high-heeled pumps and Sunday morning hats trying to keep up with the younger shoppers to grab up the best buys of the day. I finally closed my eyes when I noticed the handful of bored husbands, suited up in starched white shirts, waiting together on Bon-Ton's outside benches and bemoaning their misery in irritated unison.

The Treasured Moment: I have treasured that brief snapshot of memory for the past fifty-five years. It explains so well what I want to say in the pages of this book. Because just as my beloved grandmother offered me a haven of solitude and silence in the middle of a noisy crowd of Saturday shoppers,

Jesus offers you and me a place of refuge in the middle of a very busy society. He offers us his shoulder. Where there is disorder and noise, we can lay our heads on him and find order and peace that will transform every part of our being.

What happens when you and I leave the crowds and spend time in the Quiet Place with Christ?

"In quiet and silence the faithful soul makes progress, the hidden meanings of the Scriptures become clear, and the eyes weep with devotion…. As one learns to grow still, he draws closer to the Creator and farther from the hurly-burly of the world." (3)

How can you and I draw closer to the Creator? "Shut the door behind you…[and] call Jesus, your beloved friend, to join you. Remain with him in your cell because you won't find such peace elsewhere." (4)

Jesus' Shoulder: I have learned something significant about laying my head on Jesus' shoulder. Jesus offers us not just mental healing from the noise and chaos of the world, not just physical repair from our work and demands, not just soul renewal from our worries and problems, but a deep invigorating healing time with him. This is the deeper healing, the transforming healing, a quiet rest and communion not found anywhere else but with him. It is the peace that passes the world's understanding. When we remain with him, he gives us Living Water to drink, and his Water brings contentment, peace, and healing.

"Come to Me," he calls to us. "I am the way and the truth and the life. No one comes to the Father except through Me" (John 14:6). This type of genuine soul-healing is possible because we know that God loves us. I have no idea why he loves us, his human creation. We have moved far away from our God-image. But because God loved us, he made a way for us to come back to him, through his Son, Jesus. The relationship between God and us has been restored. It comes to us in the shape of a cross. Transformation and healing happen only through the cross of Christ.

"Man is born broken," writes Eugene O'Neill. "He lives by mending. The grace of God is glue." (5)

The very miracle of God's love for us humans keeps me in awe. It also draws me to spend time with him in solitude and silence, in close communion with the One who deeply loves me.

Your Personal Time to Reflect and Grow:

- ✓ Do you believe "exhaustion" has become the new look of the 21st century woman? Why or why not?
- ✓ Think about a time in your life when you felt truly rested. Where were you? Describe the depth of your rest. What do you remember about that time?

A Personal Prayer:

Father, thank you for loving your human creation. Thank you for opening your arms wide to receive us in communion with you. In Jesus' name, amen.

Chapter 2

Our Mind – Created for the Quiet

> "My thoughts trouble me and I am distraught….My heart is in anguish within me…. Oh, that I had the wings of a dove! I would fly away and be at rest—I would flee far away….I would hurry to my place of shelter, far from the tempest and storm." ~ Ps. 55:2-8

Our Creator gave us an incredible gift when he created our minds. D. Martyn Lloyd-Jones believes, "According to the Scripture man was made in the image of God; and a part of the image of God in man is undoubtedly the mind, the ability to think and to reason, especially in the highest sense and in a spiritual sense." (6)

I believe that God who loves us, made our minds to think and to reason and to relate to him. He also made our minds to need quiet reflection time and communion with him.

Several years ago I learned this lesson the hard way. I became mentally overwhelmed by the work of the world. Working outside the home, raising two preschoolers, maintaining a house, and keeping up with the family's depleted finances, I found myself mentally tired and unable to concentrate. I desperately needed to "escape" from the noise and pressure and work of family and society. My soul yearned for a retreat. My body longed for a few days of motionlessness. My mind craved a visit to the Quiet Place, far away from the ever-busy pace of life. I desperately needed to sit still and listen to God's gentle whisper, to meditate, to cleanse my body and soul of sound, everyday demands, and hectic confusion. I felt like King David when he cried out for the wings of a bird that he might fly away and be at peace.

The Sabbatical: Have you ever felt like this? Just bone-weary from all of life's everyday demands? Tired of the daily struggle to keep house and children and husband and finances and work going? If so, I highly suggest a short sabbatical, if possible, so that you can get away from everything and take a much-needed break and enjoy some peaceful communion time with God.

I was fortunate that year when I was overcome by weariness. I took a few days off from work, and hired some trusted help with my children. I found a quiet mountain lodge where I could be still and pray. It offered me a place with no confusion, no demands, and no interruptions. I took long walks along the hillsides. I napped when I grew tired. I spent long hours in prayer and deep thought. After a few days of solitude and silence with God, I left the lodge and traveled home. It was as if I saw my world with new eyes, and heard familiar sounds with new ears. My mind felt renewed.

During my time on the mountain, I had few distractions and prayer proved effortless, as natural as breathing. I watched the sun rise in the mornings and set in the evenings and I pondered God's creation. Somehow I found it easier to return to everyday life—the whizzing cars, blinking signs, red lights, green lights, the hypnotic glare of television tubes, meaningless radio music, and unending noise—after my short sabbatical.

Finding Quiet Time: How can you and I find quiet time, reflection time, prayer time, and healing in a society of ever-increasing chaos and noise? How can we develop a deeper relationship with God within the clamor of our everyday hectic schedules? I am convinced that we must find a way to escape the confusion, the business and busy-ness of ordinary life, so that we can enter into the Quiet Place where God waits for us, his daughters. But how do we do this? And why must we do this?

Once in a great while, we can "escape" the confusion and find a quiet mountain lodge to commune only with God. But for most women today, day-to-day routine rules out a trip to the mountains. We must somehow find our "mountain lodges" within the midst of our everyday lives. That's the beauty of the "Quiet Place." We don't have to retreat and go anywhere. We can come to the Quiet Place wherever we are, whenever we yearn for God. The Quiet Place is always within our reach. Coming to the Quiet Place means coming to Jesus.

Not long ago, I visited my good friend, Carolyn Tomlin, in Jackson, Tennessee. On the way, I stopped at the Waffle House—the busiest, noisiest restaurant on earth! I sat down in a bright orange booth and was immediately surrounded by the circus. The jukebox jumped in the background. Two cooks shouted at each other and slung dark grease on the sizzling grill in front of me. Another cracked a handful of eggs and tossed them at the stove. Weary waitresses screamed orders to the grill cooks as they slapped down raw bacon and scraped up fried hash browns. "Peeeeecan waffle! Bacon on the side! Doooooouble order hash browns! Two eggs—sunny-side-up!"

What a madhouse. A customer's cigarette smoke curled up around my cheeks. Mobs of hungry people rushed through the front door and scrambled to find a clean booth. Uncombed teenagers gobbled up sausage and eggs, then raced to their cars to reenter the highway. Kids cried loudly in the booths behind me while they waited for their breakfast. The ting-ting-ting of the cash register vibrated in my ear.

As all my five senses were over-stimulated in unison, I had an original thought. *This place is just like a miniature slice of life from the pages of the everyday world! I should be pulling out my hair. But I'm not.*

Why not? As I watched the bacon grease fly and listened to the babies cry, I mentally stepped out of that noisy waffle house and into the Quiet Place. And in all the noise and smoke and chaos, Jesus met me there. He and I communed without words; we communicated mind to mind, heart to heart. Together we watched the harried and hurried people gulp down their grits, pick up their purses, pay their bills, and scurry away like mice.

"Does he know you, Jesus?" I asked him when a young man stood to pay his bill.

"That woman is hurting, isn't she, Lord?" I asked when a stranger's face clearly revealed her secret pain.

"Jesus, please put your loving arms around that lone elderly man over there. He looks like he needs someone to love him, to care about him."

For one whole hour, Jesus and I talked, interrupted only when a waitress splashed a refill of coffee in the direction of my cup.

I decided that morning that if I could find a sense of peace and calm in that chaotic waffle house, I could find rest anywhere! I have started to come more often to the Quiet Place now, to that secret place where Jesus and I speak heart to heart. I find I can rest my mind in other challenging places, too, places where noisy activity seeks to overwhelm me—while stuck in afternoon traffic rushes, while standing in long grocery checkout lines, while listening to someone's meaningless and mindless chatter.

Sharing the Quiet: I have also found that when I freshly emerge from the restful Quiet Place, I can share the Quiet with those around me. When a tired little girl threw a temper tantrum in the middle of the grocery store pizza aisle, I surprised myself with my automatic response toward her.

I stopped my cart, and with her frazzled mother's permission, stooped to the floor, put my arms around her, and picked her up. Holding her in my arms, I smiled. The unexpected gesture of kindness immediately quieted her. Around my neck I wore a thin gold chain with a tiny mirror attached to it.

"Do you see that beautiful little girl in this mirror?" I asked her as I held the mirror up to her tear-smeared face. She caught her reflection and smiled. I slipped the necklace off my neck and onto hers. Then I gave her back to her mother. Her mother, who had stood watching this scene in utter amazement, thanked me and continued her shopping. I had been given the opportunity to share a moment of quiet and calm with an anxious little girl, and I thanked God for the unexpected experience.

Surely had I not experienced the Quiet Place myself, I couldn't have shared it with this child. I discovered in that grocery store aisle that we can only give to others what God has given first to us.

Your Personal Time to Reflect and Grow:

- ✓ Describe a time when you took a retreat to a quiet, lonely place. Where did you go? What effect did that time have on your mind?
- ✓ What happens to you mentally when you seek the Quiet Place? Have you been able to share a "moment of Quiet" with someone who needed it? Ponder the experience.

A Personal Prayer:

Father, with gratitude I thank you for time alone in communion with you. Help me to share the Quiet Place with others who need it. In Jesus' name, amen.

Chapter 3

Mind Attack!

> "Silence! What a remarkable thing that it still exists at the end of the twentieth century, here in our little meetinghouse. Moreover, these people are gathered together in the silence for a purpose: to wait upon the Lord." ~ Scott Savage, *A Plain Life* (7)

If God created our minds to be bathed and refreshed by the Quiet Place, why have we, as a society, allowed our world to become such a noisy place? Why have we filled up every silent space around us with "clanging cymbals"? These days every car has a radio, every family room has a CD and DVD player, and almost every bedroom has a personal computer and a large screen television. Noise surrounds us—in our homes, in our cars, in our culture! Certainly it hasn't always been this way.

The Judge: I chuckled not long ago when I heard about the sentencing of Edward Bello. Bello had committed some minor crime and expected to end up in jail. Instead, the judge sentenced him to nine months without television, saying he wanted "to create a condition of silent introspection" to help Bello change his behavior.

The judge ordered Bello to turn off the seven TV sets in his home. Bello's outraged lawyers called the sentence "cruel and unusual punishment"—they considered jail time to be easier! (8)

The Simpler Life: My grandparents remembered a quieter lifestyle. "Mama" and "Papa" married in 1919, and by the time Charles Lindberg had made his famous thirty-three-hour transatlantic flight, they had birthed their third and final baby—my mother. They set up their home in a small farming community atop Sand Mountain, Alabama. They used a horse and wagon for rare trips into town. They walked to Sunday morning services at their church. They grew their own food, enough for their family and for the families who lived around them—they had food to eat and food to give away. Social life was family, community, and church. They met with neighbors and fellow church members, and together ate shared covered-dish dinners, what they called "dinner on the ground."

In the evenings, they washed up the supper dishes, prepared the animals for the night, read the Bible and prayed as a family, and readied themselves and the children for bed. When darkness fell upon their small farmhouse, they said good night and went to sleep. When the sun came up the next morning, they woke, ate a hearty breakfast, dressed for the day, and set about their work. They slipped their lives into the scheduled rhythm of nature, sunrise and sunset, and lived day by day with nature's rhythms of work and rest.

My grandparents worked hard. They shared their food and their faith. They enjoyed their family and friends. They worshipped God both personally and within a congregation. They knew quiet days. They had long hours to pray while they planted and harvested their vegetable gardens, and while they canned corn and tomatoes for the lengthy winter months. They had the early evening hours of darkness to lie in bed and meditate. They allowed their minds to wonder and dream and ask questions about life and love and God. Their lives were simple, and not overwhelmed with a thousand decisions to make each hour.

Of course they had their worries and concerns during their long lives. After all, they went through a devastating Depression, two world wars, personal sickness and surgery, the deaths of parents and brothers and sisters, the problems of parenthood and grandparenthood. Yet even during their hardest days, they kept a quiet mind, a mind immersed in the quiet rituals of each day, a mind centered on Christ's constant presence.

My grandparents treasured their quiet hours. They allowed nothing, not even a newly-invented and purchased Victrola, to interrupt those God-given quiet times when they thought and prayed and pondered. Some years after the Depression, Papa bought his family a radio. They listened to the president declare war, and they used the radio to keep up with war news.

Years later they bought a black-and-white television set. For half an hour at noon, and another at night, they learned what was happening in the world news. Then the television set was shut off, and they gathered to pray for family, friends, and those hurting people spotlighted on that day's news broadcasts.

The daily habits they set in 1919, when they first established their home together, followed them throughout their lengthy lives. I remember much from my childhood about my grandparents and their small, white gabled farmhouse located then in Rossville, Georgia. I remember family socials and wonderful holiday meals and aunts and uncles and cousins. I remember long walks with Mama through her flower gardens. I remember feeding watermelon rinds to the backyard pony, Inky, and playing with the assortment of grandkids, old dogs, chickens, and one hard-boiled turkey. I remember hot summer afternoons as I sat in the kitchen and listened to the rain that interrupted my outside play.

But most of all, I remember the tranquility and the quiet. The only background noises were nature's sounds—the abrupt bark of "Little Man," the hickory nuts falling from the trees, an occasional rooster crowing, and the wind rustling autumn leaves.

Even now I often lie in bed and dream about that little farmhouse located somewhere between heaven and paradise. I retrace my steps among the backyard trees and sing the songs about Jesus my grandfather taught me. I sit on the back porch with its tin roof, and I pop green beans, fresh from the garden, with my grandmother. And I ponder our silence together, a silence broken only by the snap and tap of broken beans as they dropped into the red-rimmed, white enamel bowl.

My grandparents taught me to love the Quiet Place. For half a century, I have tried desperately to hold on to that treasured gift, a gift from the past that few children or adults today remember or cherish. The Quiet—the place for which our minds were made; the place in which are minds are mentored; the place in which our minds are re-created. God made our minds for the Quiet Place, and patiently he waits for us there, whispering softly, "Come…Come to the Quiet."

The Escape from Chaotic Contemporary Life: I hear more and more of families who yearn to return to my grandparents' simple, soundproofed way of life. Not long ago I read the fascinating story of Scott Savage and his family. Scott, along with his wife, Mary Ann, and their young children decided to leave the fast-paced American lifestyle. They made a new home with a Quaker community in Barnesville, Ohio. They gave up their car, electricity, television, radio, and all other modern conveniences. They either walk or commute around town, sometimes riding Ned, a temperamental old horse. Scott and Mary Ann have given up driver's licenses, social security cards, travel, and the hospital births of their children.

Scott finds a special joy in walking instead of driving. He learns about "the songbirds and the ditches, the bridges and the particular silhouettes of the distant hills, quietly, intimately, as only the walkers of the world experience." He has discovered that walking "leaves me feeling I have exited time to participate in the eternal 'now' of creation. It puts me in a relationship of reverie and praise for all I see." (9)

After living with silence in the Quaker community, the Savages took their children on a train ride to learn about their local history. While standing in a line of loud, noisy people from outside the Quaker community, Scott reflects: "The differences in behavior and appearance encountered in the larger world have come to seem ever more amazing and bizarre." (10)

Learning the Secrets of Solitude and Silence

Your Personal Time to Reflect and Grow:

- ✓ Describe the noise level in your home. What steps can you personally take to make it a quieter place?
- ✓ Explain what happened to Scott and Mary Ann when they gave up their complicated lives and moved into a quiet Quaker community. Have you ever wanted to leave the "world" behind and find a quieter place to live? What kinds of things did Scott notice when he gave up his car and started to walk?

A Personal Prayer:

Lord, help us as we live in a world of noise and yearn for the Quiet Place. Show us how to find quiet time in our present restless society. In Jesus name, amen.

Chapter 4

Resting Our Mind in Christ

"It doesn't require a Ph.D. from Princeton to assess that we are busy, busy, busy. Forever on the move, doing things, eating stuff, working, jumping, jogging, writing, marrying, divorcing, buying...you name it, our country is doing it.... The pace is somewhere between maddening and insane. The freeways are shocked with traffic, people are going or coming twenty-four hours every day...with no letup in sight. Faces reflect tension. The air is polluted. The earth shakes. The malls are crowded. Nerves are shot."
~ Charles Swindoll (11)

How can you and I find the Quiet Place—the place of worship, reverence, and awe—escaping the place located "somewhere between maddening and insane"—when our minds have been conditioned by artificial techno-noise, when "our brains are no longer conditioned for reverence and awe?" (12)

Over the past fifty years or so, television and the media, not creative and worshipful silence, have molded our minds, zapped our attention spans, and glazed over our eyes. The change from quiet to chaos, by the television media, came slowly and over time.

"First radio, then television, have assaulted and overturned the privacy of the home, the real American privacy, which permitted the development of a higher and more independent life within democratic society. Parents can no longer control the atmosphere of the home and have lost even the will to do so." (13)

Let's Get Practical: How can we celebrate solitude when our weary minds are constantly surrounded and assaulted by chaos? Here are some practical suggestions that have worked for me and for others, and that might work for you, too.

- ❖ **Television.** Turn off the television set. I've been in some homes where the TV stays on all day and all evening. TV had become like an adopted member of the family! Television can become a noisy, time-eating habit. Plan the programs you want to watch. Before the programs begin, and after the programs end, keep the television turned off. We get so used to television background noise, we are no longer even aware of it. We don't need the constant background chatter. Larry Burkett writes about the effects of television on the minds of today's children: "The net result is a nearly brain-dead generation of kids growing up on the garbage dished out by the most liberal segment of our society: the media. There are some good things on TV, but you have to pick and choose carefully for your kids and for yourself as well." (14)
- ❖ **Special Places.** Find a special place in your home or garden or office where you can escape for a few minutes of solitude during the day. It may be a favorite chair in your bedroom. Or a bench in your garden. Or a couch in the ladies' room at your office building. Any place will do, as long as you can enjoy a moment of Quiet alone. When you visit your place of Quiet, sit in silence for a few minutes. In doing so, you will be taking a break from the noise pollution that constantly surrounds you. Visit your Quiet Place as often as you can. These moments will refresh your mind.
- ❖ **Time Out Noise.** When you cannot "escape" to a place of Quiet, learn how to tune out the noise around you.

- Think about the most lovely place you've ever been.
- Lose yourself by looking at a restful painting of a nature scene.
- Relax your body.
- Breathe deeply.
- Concentrate mentally on the One who loves you, the One who gave himself for you. Be aware of him, for he stands beside you.
- Surround your workplace with meaningful and beautiful things such as flowers and pictures and pottery.

Benefits of the Quiet Place: In doing so, you will be resisting the work of the enemy Noise. Did you know that recent studies on "noise pollution" state that noise can cause certain health problems, such as cardiovascular disease, impaired speech ability, increased blood pressure and stress hormone levels, sleep disturbance, etc.? Ordinary environmental noise can cause a variety of symptoms, including anxiety, emotional stress, nervous complaints, nausea, headaches, instability, argumentativeness, sexual impotency, changes in mood, increase in social conflicts, and general psychiatric disorders such as neurosis, psychosis, and hysteria. High levels of environmental noise can cause deteriorated mental health. Noise can have the most damaging effect on the elderly, ill, or depressed; people with particular diseases or medical problems; people dealing with complex cognitive tasks; the blind and hearing-impaired; fetuses, babies, and young children. High-level, continuous noise can contribute to "feelings of helplessness" among school children. (15)

Resist Distractions: Author Catherine Marshall advises people to "shut out distractions—the doorbell, the telephone, the [delivery person], the children [playing].... God asks that we worship Him with concentrated minds... A divided and scattered mind is not at its most receptive." (16)

Learning the Secrets of Solitude and Silence

- **Make This Your Daily Prayer:** *Lord, God, there is so much noise in my world, in my life, that makes it difficult to hear my own inner thoughts, let alone listen to the Words of your beloved Son. Help me to acquire the kind of inner peace that will open my being to your Word so that I can respond appropriately.* (17)
- **Recite Scripture:** During stressful times, close your eyes and recite from memory a favorite Bible verse. Strive to memorize those verses that will bring you peace and calm to your overworked mind.
- **Pray Constantly:** It takes only seconds to tell the Lord that you love him. Pray sentence prayers throughout your busy days. Constant prayer will keep your mind constantly on Christ.
- **Mentally Vacate:** Plan mental vacations. Choose a morning or afternoon, and plan to sit and ponder alone quietly. Use this time of solitude to think about your life and its priorities. Think about your faith. Count your blessings. Pray aloud without interruptions. A morning and/or afternoon spent in the Quiet Place with Jesus will fill you deeply with his refreshing Living Water.
- **Go to the Library:** Visit your local community library as often as you can. It's usually quiet there. In fact, the library remains one of the few places society gives us that offer silence instead of noise. Give yourself time to browse through the rows of books. Sit. Read. Lose yourself in classic and contemporary works. Join the thoughts and experiences of authors of yesterday and today. Check out books. Plan quiet times during your busy days at home to read.
- **Spend Time at a Church:** If possible, walk to a nearby church during your lunch hour on your busy workdays. Find a comfortable pew. Spend a few moments in the Quiet to pray.
- **Expect Quiet Consideration at Home:** Ask family members to be quieter at home. Teach children to

speak more softly indoors. Keep television, radio, computers, and other noisy devices at a lower volume, or turned off. Practice being quieter as a family.

- **Rise Early:** Get up earlier on some mornings. Enjoy the Quiet and solitude. Sit in the dark with your eyes closed. Listen to your breathing. Take this time to thank God for your mind and for your God-given ability to think and ponder and pray. Thank him for your wonderfully created body. Thank him for family and friends. Praise him with thanksgiving for all his many gifts of blessing to you and your family.
- **Resist Worrying:** Worry can become a habit. Give your worries to God and allow your mind to take a vacation from worry. Ask him to settle your mind, and recite this wonderful Scripture verse whenever you feel overly-concerned: *Do not be anxious about anything, but in everything, by prayer and petition, with thanksgiving present your requests to God. [Then enjoy] the peace of God, which transcends all understanding, [which] will guard your hearts and your minds in Christ Jesus.* (Philippians 4:6-7)
- **Monitor Your Thoughts:** The Apostle Paul gives us wonderful advice about our thoughts. He tells us: *Whatever is true, whatever is noble, whatever is right, whatever is pure, whatever is lovely, whatever is admirable—if anything is excellent or praiseworthy—think about these things.* (Philippians 4:8)
- **Rest Your Brain:** In order to operate at peak performance and to learn/remember new skills, our brain needs its rest. Dr. Sara C. Mednick, a Harvard psychologist, writes about a new study on mind and rest and learning: "The brain needs sleep to incorporate newly learned skills into the permanent memory." (18) Take naps! Find time to clear your mind and let your brain renew itself.

No doubt you have many ideas of your own about how to bring delightful peace and quiet into daily chaos and how to eliminate unnecessary noise from your office and home. These are but a few suggestions. Remember that God created our minds for quiet. Our minds need regular rest from worries, stress, and the pressures of noise and daily life.

Heed the call of Jesus when he calls you to "Come...Come to the Quiet Place." He has much to say to you and me. He has much to teach us in the Quiet Place with him. He wants to fill our minds with his refreshing Living Water. He wants to enrich our minds with his wisdom, his Word, and his encouragement. Come to the Quiet Place. He waits for you there. Listen to him speak to you. After a few minutes with him in the Quiet Place, you'll step back into the bustling world with a changed mind, a mind that Christ himself will begin to transform.

Your Personal Time to Reflect and Grow:

- ✓ What does it mean to "rest your mind in Christ"?
- ✓ What advice does Paul give us in Philippians 4:8? Why is this advice important?

A Personal Prayer:

Father, show me how to spend more time with you in the Quiet Place, how to rest my mind in Christ and find healing and mind-renewal. In Jesus' name, amen.

Chapter 5

Letting Christ Transform Our Mind

"A whole person lies inside the bony box, locked in, protected, sealed away from the indispensable duties of managing one hundred trillion cells in a human body. The Head of the Body is the seat of mystery and wisdom and unity." (19)

Surely there is nothing on earth so wonderful as the human mind that God created and set within our "bony box"! The three-pound human brain, five hundred million times more complicated than our most advanced computer, is being called 'the new frontier.'" (20)

Who can fathom its intricate, complex design? Eric Chaisson, who received his doctorate in astrophysics from Harvard University, has described the human brain as "the most exquisitely complex clump of matter in the known universe." (21)

Did you know that you keep the neurons or nerve cells of your mind throughout your whole life? All your other cells age and are replaced about every seven years. Your skin, eyes, heart, and bones are entirely different today from those you carried around just one decade ago. But what makes you YOU—your brain—stays the same, "maintaining the continuity of selfhood that keeps the entity of [YOU] alive." (22)

The Amazing Miracle!: Your mind is an amazing miracle! Scripture tells us, "Let this mind be in you which was also in Christ Jesus" (Philippians 2:5 KJV). In other words, Paul tells us to become "Christ-minded"; we are to follow Christ into the Quiet with our minds. Several things happen to our minds when we do this.

As you and I spend time with Christ, we become more like him. As our mind rests in Christ, we regain our sense of awe and reverence, of worship and wonder. Becoming Christ-minded means that we begin to think like Jesus Christ himself. We think his thoughts. He fills our minds with his words. He teaches us to discern more clearly his gentle whisper. We learn to recognize his voice when he speaks our names and calls us to the Quiet Place to be with him.

Author Henri Nouwen writes: "Once we have committed ourselves to spending time in solitude, we develop an attentiveness to God's voice in us." (23)

The more time we spend with Christ in the Quiet Place, the more in tune with him our minds become. We hear him. We develop a deeper awareness of God's presence weaving throughout the ordinary hours of our lives. We begin to see the world around us through his eyes. Our worldview conforms to his worldview. We see other people as Jesus sees them. We peer beneath the "masks" people wear. We look deep into their hearts and minds and learn their pains and concerns. We learn to "read between the lines" of a person's life and speech. Christ enables us to better reach out to help those around us who are hurting. We experience compassion; we learn to empathize, to identify with, and to suffer with the wounded of this world.

Appreciating the Quiet: As we spend time with Christ in the Quiet Place, we learn to better appreciate the Quiet. We come to crave the Quiet as an animal craves water on a hot, dry day. The more time we spend in the Quiet Place, the more time we will want to spend there.

When we reduce the volume of noise around us, we will begin to hear sounds we haven't heard before. Softer sounds will delight us. Sounds like the heartfelt question a small child asks. Or the peeping of newly hatched birds in a nest. Or soft winds blowing through tree branches on a gentle day. Or crickets chirping at night under our bedroom window. Or the sound a stream makes as it flows over smooth rocks. When we immerse ourselves in the Quiet Place, we will learn how to truly listen and hear.

The Deeper Things: The Quiet Place creates within our minds a keener sense of concentration when we give ourselves time to contemplate. Gone will be surface thoughts. Our thoughts will run much deeper, and our conversations will become more meaningful. We will take nothing at face value anymore. We will ponder the deeper meanings of another's unexpected action or careless word. What might have once upset us will no longer hold such irritating power over us. We will become more like Jesus in our actions. We will move through life as he did, with keener concentration, deeper concern for others; mind and motions will be unhurried, unfettered, no longer so anxious.

Transformation begins in the mind. Transformation begins in the Quiet Place, when we set aside serious time to listen to the voice of God. Paul tells us about mind transformation when he writes, "Do not conform any longer to the pattern of this world, but be transformed by the renewing of your *mind*" (Romans 12:2).

What is the Quiet Place? It is Christ. The Quiet is the place of solitude where we can come to Christ, rest our minds, and request mental transformation and healing.

Paul urges, "Let this mind be in you, which was also in Christ Jesus, who, being in the form of God…took upon him the form of a servant and was made in the likeness of men" (Philippians 2:5-7 KJV).

Where is the Quiet Place? It's anywhere you want it to be.

It's the black Chevrolet and a grandmother's shoulder; it's a lonely lodge on a mountainside; it's Jackson, Tennessee's waffle-eating people with tired, weary faces; it's a prayerful Quaker meetinghouse and a temperamental old horse named Ned.

The Quiet Place is a mind set on Christ, and Christ alone. Surely those who live in accordance with the Spirit have their minds set on what the Spirit desires (see Romans 8:5). "You will keep in perfect peace him whose mind is steadfast, because he trusts in you," writes Isaiah (26:3). "The mind controlled by the Spirit is life and peace" (see Romans 8:6).

"Come to me," Jesus invites. "Come to me, all you who are weary and burdened, and I will give you rest" (Matthew 11:28).

What wonderful promises!

Your Personal Time to Reflect and Grow:

- ✓ Reflect on what you have learned from this study of your mind and its need for quiet, calm, peace, and transformation.
- ✓ Paul writes, "Let this mind be in you, which was also in Christ Jesus." What do you think he means by this statement?

A Personal Prayer:

Father, I come to the Quiet Place needing mental rest, renewal, and communion with you. I pray for the mind-transformation that only you can bring. In Jesus' name, I pray, amen.

Section 2

Healing
the Body

"Come to Me, all who labor…"
~ Matthew 11:28 NKJV

Chapter 6

Today's Woman – Overworked!

> Karl Rahner speaks for many exhausted women in this nation when he laments: "How can I redeem this wretched humdrum? …How can I escape from the prison of this routine? …Wasn't I already deeply entangled in the pettiness of every day cares, when it first dawned on me that I must not allow myself to be suffocated under the weight of earthly routine? …I myself have dug the rut…. My days don't make me dull—it's the other way around…. I realize that we gradually get tired of the feverish activity that seems so important to a young mind and heart."
> ~ Karl Rahner (24)

If you love your job, have plenty of quality time with your husband, kids, and friends, are satisfied with your time for home keeping duties, and enjoy ample personal, quiet, devotional time with God, then you can skip this chapter—you don't need it! In fact, you should be writing this book! You are Superwoman, a rare and endangered species.

However, if you are one of the millions of women in this country who work too hard, are physically exhausted and stressed-out, have little quality time with your husband, kids, or friends, stay far behind in your housework, and have little or no quiet time for solitude and prayer, then keep reading. I wrote this chapter—and this book—just for you.

Perhaps you can identify with my friend Janice. Janice had tears streaming down her face when she confessed to me: "Denise, I feel like I'm on a treadmill. I work as hard as I can, and I still can't get everything done. I'm missing important deadlines at the office, my house is a mess, and my husband and kids are getting the worst leftover part of me at night. I come home from work each afternoon exhausted. I give what little energy I have left to my family. After I put the kids to bed at night, I have nothing left for my husband. I can tell you this: I can't keep this schedule much longer. It's just not working anymore! It's robbing all the joy from my life. What can I do?"

Janice stopped talking and looked at me as if she expected me to instantly give her the perfect solution to her problems. I like Janice; we have been good friends for years. At the time, she had a high-profile job in a downtown law firm, a wonderful Christian husband, and three school-aged daughters.

In my heart, I wanted to ask her some brutally hard questions, questions I had struggled to answer just a few years earlier. But I bit my tongue. I didn't want to overstep the boundaries of our friendship. I told her this was a personal situation about which she must pray, ponder deeply, and make some definite decisions.

I simply told her, "No one but God can guide you and your family in making these choices. Only he knows what you and your family need." Even so, I assured Janice I would pray for her as she sought the Lord's advice. I also suggested that she talk with a Christian counselor, a person who could look at her situation objectively, and then honestly discuss it with her.

"Look at the big picture of your life," I urged. "Pray diligently for God's guidance. Consider the needs of your family as well as your own physical and spiritual needs."

The Heart Questions: What were the "heart questions" I yearned to ask her—those painfully direct questions about her life, her work, her faith, her family, and her priorities? Those questions God had directly pointed out to me? Here are some of them:

- ❖ "Exactly why are you working outside the home, Janice, when you could simplify your lifestyle and live without the extra income?"
- ❖ "Are you really physically able to continue this chaotic schedule, and if so, are you somehow harming your future health? Is the extra income you make worth the physical risks to your health?"
- ❖ "Have you somehow confused your work with your self-worth? Does your self-esteem come from your position, paycheck, and impressive credentials?"
- ❖ "Are you willing to possibly sacrifice your marriage and children for your work goals? Is full-time employment strangling your family time, and if so, is the trade-off worth it?"
- ❖ "What are you teaching your daughters about life and faith priorities? Do you want them to follow in your hassled, hurried footsteps? What kind of example are you setting for them?"

These are tough questions. For some women, they have no choice about whether to work outside the home or not. But, for others, like Janice, they could stop working and still survive financially.

If I had asked Janice these questions, I can only imagine what her answers would be. Janice had bought into the myth that women can do everything, and do everything perfectly: work a demanding full-time job, keep a beautiful, clean home, birth and rear children, keep a busy husband satisfied, grow her own herbs and vegetables, and play a great game of competitive tennis! And always look good and never complain of exhaustion.

Janice has been a woman swept along with the current American tide of "having it all, doing it all." She graduated from college and then graduate school, found a good job, married, had children, and never questioned her choice to work outside her home. Now after a few years of reality, demanding responsibilities, she fights exhaustion, frustration with her own physical limitations, spiritual dryness, and loss of joy.

Just Work Harder?!: To stay abreast of current legal information and trends, Janice found herself working harder and longer hours both at the office and at home. Her work hours gobbled up almost her entire family and personal time. Janice was completely wrapped up in her job; in fact, she had *become* her work. Her prestigious position became the fragile vessel that held her self-esteem. She believed her position gave her worth as a woman. In the meantime, Janice lived on the "treadmill," always running, always in a hurry, always too busy to kick off her shoes and escape into solitude and silence. I knew it was just a matter of time before Janice wore out. And so did she.

Our Imaginary Conversation: As I drove home from Janice's house, I had an imaginary dialogue with her. One by one, I asked her the questions that lay so heavy on my heart. I could almost predict her answers.

> ***Denise:*** *"Exactly why are you working outside the home, Janice, when you don't necessarily need the extra income?"*
>
> ***Janice:*** *"That's just what I do! I've never considered not working. Anyway, there's nothing wrong with working outside the home. I'm good at what I do. I like to have extra money to buy the luxuries I want. I can give my kids so much more than I had as a kid. And anyway, I spent too many years in graduate school learning this profession to quit my job and waste my talents."*
>
> ***Denise***: *"Is the extra money worth your health? Are you really physically able to continue this chaotic schedule, and, if so, are you somehow harming your future health?"*
>
> ***Janice:*** *"I have to admit, Denise, that this schedule is killing*

me! The constant exhaustion is beginning to be a real problem now. I don't know how long I can keep this pace, but the alternative is to quit my job. I guess I could live without the extra money. But I don't want to quit! It's who I am, what I do. I don't know any other lifestyle."

Denise: "Janice, have you somehow confused your work with your worth as a woman? Does your self-esteem come from your position, paycheck, and impressive credentials?" I yearned to tell Janice that: "God has to be the source of your self-esteem and how you view yourself as a woman. Looking to another human being, or to a cultural movement… [or anything else!] …for your inner peace and sense of worth will always result in disappointment." (26)

Janice: "Now, Denise, that's a personal question. I'd like to think about that one for a while. But I guess I am possibly too proud of my position, the size of my paycheck, and yes, my credentials are impressive. But they are impressive because I have worked extremely hard in a competitive field. They have not come easily! But surely I don't consider my self-worth to come from my job…uh…do I?"

Denise: "Janice, are you willing to possibly sacrifice your marriage and children to your work goals?"

Janice: "Come on, Denise! I don't think I'm sacrificing my husband and children because I work an outside job! That sounds like an insult. I wouldn't purposely hurt my family. But I do feel that I just don't have enough time with them. We rush through supper, hurry through homework, and we don't have much evening time to talk and play together. To tell you the truth, I miss having down time with them. They're growing up so quickly, and I'm not with them as much as I'd like to be. As for my husband, he works hard too. That's the American way, isn't it? We both want to do well. Yet I guess I have to admit that I miss him too. We try to have family devotions at supper—you *know, Bible reading and prayer—but with homework, extra office work, soccer practice, and piano lessons—sometimes we just can't squeeze it in."*

Denise: *"What are you teaching your daughters about life and faith priorities? Do you want them to follow in your hassled, hurried footsteps? What kind of example are you setting for them?"*

Janice: *"That cuts to the bone, Denise! My answer is NO, NO, NO!! I certainly don't want my daughters to work all the time, always be behind in their schedules, never have time for themselves or their families, and lose the very joy of living. I don't want my grandchildren to have mothers who don't have time for them because of some demanding full-time job. But here again, I want my girls to be successful, have high self-esteem, and have a purpose for their lives."*

I pray that one day Janice will figure it out, that she will learn to listen to her exhausted physical body, that she will give herself needed time to spend resting in the Quiet Place, and that she will set her priorities in order.

Maybe...with God's help...she will look at the big picture of her life, ask herself some tough personal questions, and then make life-changing choices that will enrich her own life as well as that of her family.

I also yearn to remind Janice that life is short. I have lost too many friends to death, friends that learned too late just how temporary human life can be. "The future is now," I want to tell Janice. "You may not have a tomorrow. Figure out what is essential, important, and necessary, and then make life changes."

Listen to the words of the psalmist: "Remember how fleeting is my life" (Psalm 89:47). Heed Scripture and pray with the psalmist: "Teach us to number our days aright, that we may gain a heart of wisdom" (Psalm 90:12).

Learning the Secrets of Solitude and Silence

What I Long to Shout From the Rooftops!: Perhaps you are like Janice. I certainly used to be. You work too hard. You run yourself ragged. Your body is always exhausted. Too much to do, too busy to seek solitude, never any time for yourself, little time and energy for your family, no daydream time, no lunches with friends, etc.

Have you ever stopped to ask yourself why you feel you must do everything you do? Yes, we all have work to do. Work is good. Work is rewarding. Work is necessary. But are you spreading yourself so thin that you are doing nothing as well as you would like to? Have you lost your joy of living? Are you "all work" and "no play"? Are you living in a rut, in the bottom of a deep, dull pit?

Whenever I meet a person like Janice, whenever I hear her inward heart's cry and her outward verbal frustration, I silently pray for her. Then I ask her to stop, put her hand on her heart, and quietly listen.

I'd like to say the same thing to you right now. Stop reading, take a deep breath, and place your hand over your heart. Quietly listen. Your heart knows a secret that most American women have never learned. God created your heart to beat and then to rest. Beat and rest. Beat and rest. Imagine what would happen to your heart, to your entire body, if your heart beat (worked) constantly and never stopped to rest! It would wear out in a very short time. Your heart works and rests in perfect harmony. It gives equal time to both work and rest. I believe this is the way God created your body—to work and rest, work and rest, in equal parts, in perfect harmony. Your heart knows what makes life balanced, an equal portion of work and rest. Will you stop and listen to the message of your heart?

Redeeming the Humdrum: "How can I redeem this wretched humdrum? ...How can I escape from the prison of this routine?... I realize that we gradually get tired of the feverish activity that seems so important to a young mind and heart." (25)

Perhaps accumulated age and wisdom help many women to seriously think through their priorities, to push away the feverish activity that seemed so important in their younger years. Maybe it's the wretched humdrum and the weight of routine that wakes us up to stop and think about the really important things of life. Perhaps it is the entanglement of the petty everyday cares that stirs a woman's heart to number her days and think carefully about how best to fill them.

Sometimes women have little choice about their daily routine. I know of two single mothers that have autistic children. I know of other women who must work difficult jobs to feed their children and put a roof over their heads. In these days of economic strains, women may not have a choice about some of the things they do and jobs they work.

But I meet so many women today who, like Janice, do have a choice. And they are choosing to be Superwoman! They want to do everything, and do it all perfectly. They involve themselves in meaningless projects, spends hours like precious gold on things that have little eternal significance. I want to tell them, please stop, go to the Quiet Place, meet with God and pray about all those things you currently do. Ponder their significance. View them in light of the temporary and the eternal. For what are you trading the precious hours of your limited life?

Thinking through Our Priorities: On the one hand, we, as women, are fortunate to have as many choices as we do in modern society. Women in the past haven't had the educational and/or job opportunities we now enjoy.

On the other hand, more choices mean we have more decisions to make about those choices. Making decisions about work and employment often prove difficult. When a Christian woman decides to discontinue outside employment and have more time for herself and her family, she will find that she must carefully control her involvement in other activities. It's not only employment that can eat away our personal, family, and prayer time. Community charities, schools, and churches can quickly consume our precious time with their unending (and often unnecessary) requests for our participation. We must make our priority lists even when we are work-at-home women. Otherwise we will allow others to deplete our time and energy with their expectations as much (or even more so) than a full time job would.

"Actions that lead to overwork, exhaustion, and burnout can't praise and glorify God. What God calls us to do we can do and do well. When we listen in silence to God's voice and speak with our friends in trust we will know what we are called to do and we will do it with a grateful heart." (27)

More and more, however, our nation is watching working women make tough decisions to "go against the tide of society," give away their briefcases, admit they need time for their top priorities in life, and leave outside jobs. For women who must work, such as single women, moms, widows, and those financially overextended, many are rethinking exhausting work habits, finding alternatives to eight hours at the office each day and congested commutes, and meeting with financial planners who help them plan futures without full time employment.

It's about time.

Your Personal Time to Reflect and Grow:

- ✓ Ponder the activities you do. Ask God to show you what to keep and what to give up.
- ✓ From what source do you personally derive your sense of self-worth?
- ✓ Can you personally relate to the issues surrounding women and work? Do you try to live under the unrealistic American "have it all, do it all" expectations for women today? What are your options? What decisions can you make to improve your life?

A Personal Prayer:

Father, show me the eternal significance of my work, and help me to know what I should keep doing and what I should give up for better things. In Jesus' name, amen.

Chapter 7

Stress Attack!

> "Modern people lack silence. They no longer lead their own lives; they are dragged along by events. It is a race against the clock." ~ Dr. Paul Tournier (28)

This "race against the clock" has produced an epidemic in the United States, as well as other countries—the sad state of "dis-stress."

What is stress? It's certainly not a new problem. Reams have been written over the years about stress and its effects on the human body. Stress can be good or bad. Good stress (*eu-stress*) gets us out of bed in the mornings and helps us start our day. Bad stress (*dis-stress*), in overwhelming portions, can put us back into bed and make us sick.

The late Dr. Wayne E. Oates, my friend and seminary professor, explains:

"Stress is like heat in your body or in the engine of your automobile. Some of it is vitally necessary to the proper function of your body or your car. Too little or too much is equally threatening. An effective balance must be maintained." (29)

We have become a society of stressed-out women, women who juggle too many plates in the air at the same time, women who are overwhelmed by everyday stress, women who have failed to find that "effective balance" between work and solitude.

Anne Morrow Lindbergh wrote back in 1965 about the problem of *dis-stress*:

"The world is rumbling and erupting in ever-widening circles around us. The tensions, conflicts and sufferings even in the outermost circle touch us all... Modern communication loads us with more problems than the human frame can carry. (30)

What would Mrs. Lindbergh think now on the eve of 2012?! She really wouldn't believe what has happened to us in just a few short years! Over-stress in the twenty-first century has become almost unbearable! And it is hurting us now more than ever before.

Crisis Stress: Crisis stress happens when we face an unexpected accident or emergency. We discover hidden physical strengths we didn't know we had. This rugged inner power springs to heart and soul and fortifies us physically when we must face and endure life's crises. When my father died, I watched my mother become a tower of strength. With focused energy she arranged a funeral, comforted remaining family members, and took care of reams of necessary paper work. She knew what had to be done, and she took it on with some mysterious innate energy and ability.

Newscasters routinely tell us of women who perform super-natural feats of strength and power and sheer will when they face a severe crisis. We honor people who exhibit extraordinary strength and courage in times of disaster, like that shown during and after terrorists destroyed the World Trade Centers on September 11, 2001.

As you and I are faced with life's crises, we find that we can usually deal with a house fire or a tornado or a car wreck or a loved one's death when it happens suddenly. These out-of-the-ordinary events pull from our hidden strengths. These are our reserve physical powers that ordinarily lie untapped unless they are confronted with catastrophe.

Let me give you an example. You are outside tending to your flower garden. All of a sudden, out of the woods, a bear comes toward you. You must instantly make a life-saving decision, and your body prepares to help you. "Should I fight the bear?" "Or should I take flight and run away from it?" In these brief seconds of crisis stress, your body automatically prepares to fight or to flee. It is an innate survival reaction built into the human body by the Creator. It helps keep us alive when we face enemy threats.

Inside Your Body: What happens inside your body when you face the bear and know your life is in danger? Your heart races and your blood pressure soars to increase the flow of blood to your brain. You have a life and death decision to make, and the extra blood to your head will improve your decision-making faculties. Your blood sugar rises, furnishing you with more fuel for physical energy. Blood from your gut will be ordered to the large muscles of your arms and legs. You will need increased speed and strength to either fight the bear or run away from it. The blood arranges quicker clotting in case the bear tears your skin or causes you to hemorrhage internally.

Within seconds your body supplies you with extraordinary strength and helps you to save your life or the lives of others.

People expect us to suffer intense stress, to the point of collapse, when tough events and neighborhood bears suddenly face us. We give ourselves permission to take the needed time to mend, heal, grieve, and rebuild. Everyone understands the reason we are failing to cope well with life—we've had a frightening, draining experience-shock. They expect us to need love and care, time and space to recover. They give hands-on physical help to bring us through the crisis stress. Most people have, themselves, experienced tragedy. They know only too well how life's inevitable catastrophes can knock us off our feet.

But consider this: The everyday, small, repeating stresses of life can also knock us off our feet! These daily aggravations—our "races against the clock"—can make us sick. They can quickly accumulate on top of each other and become deadly to our physical health. They can do the same kind of damage to our body that an unexpected and frightening bear attack can do. It's like water dripping onto a rock. After a while, the tiny drops of water will wear down the strong sturdy rock.

The Problem of Everyday Stress: "If you are operating on stress overload, you can expect to become sick. Irritating daily hassles can wear you down like a car engine racing at full throttle with the emergency brake on. You can expect to become just as ill with these repeated, daily aggravations as you would from major, life-changing traumas." (31)

Life's little irritations—those constant daily hassles—can produce the same physical responses for survival as those we discover when we encounter a bear! The mind becomes alert. The heart races and sends extra blood to the muscles. The alerted muscles flex with extra strength.

But in the bear attack, the grizzly strikes and then leaves. Your body then becomes normal again. But in everyday stress, the "grizzly" stays. The bear continues to frighten you and to threaten your life. Your mind, heart, and muscles stay on continual alert. They remain at complete attention, armed and ready to fight or flee from the enemy. The "enemy," though, never goes away. Day after day after day, overstress keeps you in anticipation of the bear's attack. You live every day of your life with your body screaming: "Okay! Call it quick! Do I fight or do I flee?!"

These wonderful life-saving physical stress responders deal well with the occasional bear attack. Yet the stress that plagues women today is not generally a dangerous confrontation with a wild beast, but "rather a host of emotional threats like getting stuck in traffic and fights with customers, co-workers, or family members, that often occur several times a day." (32) Our bodies prepare physically for a temporary attack, but without relief, these fight-or-flight responses "are now not only not useful but potentially damaging and deadly. Repeatedly invoked, it is not hard to see how they can contribute to hypertension, strokes, heart attacks, diabetes, ulcers, neck or low back pain and other 'diseases of civilization.'" (33)

When we can find no relief from these everyday stresses, they tend to multiply. We become touchy with our husband. We respond more adversely to the little annoyances caused by our kids. We become overly frustrated with ourselves. The least added stress—such as a "simple criticism" from a loved one (if there is such a thing!)—can send us crashing into tears, or worse, into fists.

Dr. Paul Brand writes: "When we are under severe strain, maybe resulting from an accumulation of small stresses—bills, work pressures, irritating habits of family members—suddenly every minor frustration hits like a blow. We have become hypersensitive, and our minds are telling us we need a respite as surely as neuronal hypersensitivity warns our bodies of a need for relief." (34)

Medical science has known for years what the "accumulation of small stresses" can do to our bodies. Doctors have linked over-stress to "the development and course of cancer, high blood pressure, heart attacks, diabetes, asthma, allergies, ulcers, colitis, alcoholism, smoking, obesity, headaches, backaches, and many other diseases." (35)

As hard as it is to believe, the stacking up of everyday stresses, day after day, can be just as hazardous to our health as a major catastrophe!

"Most researchers today accept that major stressful events do indeed take a toll on health. But the latest research suggests that the average person is as likely to be 'nibbled to death' by everyday hassles as overwhelmed by tragedies." (36)

It's no wonder that women today are suffering from increased heart attacks! Did you know that "women account for about one-third of patients who undergo procedures (such as *percutaneous* coronary interventions) to clear the clogged arteries causing a heart attack?" (37) In fact, each year, heart disease claims the lives of more women than breast cancer and lung cancer combined! (38)

Do you feel "nibbled to death by everyday hassles"? Do you feel dragged along by events that seem out of your control? When is the last time you trekked to the Quiet Place and spent some solitary and silent time with God?

Your Personal Time to Reflect and Grow:

- ✓ What is your definition of "stress"? What is the difference between "crisis stress" and "everyday stress"?
- ✓ What are those pressures in your life right now that send you into feelings of *dis-stress*?

A Personal Prayer:

Father, help me to monitor my stress levels to keep them from nibbling me to death. Show me what you want me to do. In Jesus' name, amen.

Chapter 8

Job Stress

"Trust in the Lord with all your heart and lean not on your own understanding; in all your ways acknowledge him, and he will make your paths straight." ~ Proverbs 3:5-6 NIV

Much of a full time employed woman's everyday stress is brought on in the workplace. This is especially true for the working mother who holds down a full time job, helps her husband, and rears her children. The stress multiplies when the working mother is single and must financially support and raise her children alone. On the average, working moms work too hard, labor too many hours in a single day, get minimal sleep at night, and have little or no occasion to rest during the day. Today's working mother is sleep-starved, and she is at high risk for stress-related diseases.

Job Stress: What is job stress? The experts tell us that work pressures are far and away the leading source of stress for American adults. Job stress has been steadily increasing over the past few decades. Job stress is also a problem when a worker has lost her job, needs the income to survive, and is out walking the pavement trying to find a new job!

Overwork, fatigue, expectations from others, and many other work-related issues can contribute to unrelenting everyday stress.

They can make a woman sick.

Some women complain about the commute to and from a job. For the hours you spend commuting each day, you are bombarded with traffic noise, road rage, tension, and potential accidents. It's no wonder that many women are physically exhausted and emotionally tense by the time they arrive at work. After a full day of overwork and long hours, a woman must still face the difficult commute back to her home. Whether she drives, takes the train, subway, or bus, the tension and tiredness brought about by after-work commute pressures can take a definite toll on family life that evening.

Most employed women also might keep up a home—including housework, house repair, and yard work. They say that causes as much stress as outside employment. Keeping a house running properly requires huge amounts of energy and resourcefulness. It's a full time job in itself.

Home and family record-keeping is also stressful. Many married women I know take on this vital role in their households. Most single moms have no choice but to handle record-keeping, car payments, house mortgages, utility expenses, life- and car- and house-insurance payments, retirement accounts, social security benefits, medical insurance premiums, checking and saving accounts—the list goes on and on. They pay the bills, pay repair people, and prepare the income tax forms.

Employment, commute, housework, and the rigors of routine record-keeping can keep a woman overwhelmed.

And to this workload, many women add parenting and grand parenting. Children bring big blessings to our lives—there's no doubt about it. But children also bring huge amounts of additional work to our daily schedules. Many women today, who have already "emptied" their nests of their own children, are now taking on the responsibility of raising their grandchildren full time. Women are also discovering that fully-grown children, who have already left the nest, often fly back to live there. They move right back into their own childhood bedrooms. Sometimes they even bring a wife and children!

Additional Work Added: Of course we love our children and grandchildren! We welcome their visits. We cherish our times together. They are truly God's gifts to us. But additional family members mean additional meals to prepare, clothes to launder, bills to pay, groceries to buy—more physical work and less physical rest.

Women today also must deal with out-of-the-ordinary stress issues. Consider women caught in the "sandwich" generation. At the same time they are raising teenagers, they are also taking care of aging and/or ill parents. They are teaching their teens to drive while making sure their parents take the correct medications. They are dealing with their child's dating dilemmas as well as transporting elderly in-laws to doctor's appointments and sleeping next to them in hospital rooms.

Most women handle their everyday stressors well enough. They keep up, make an honest effort to get everything done, and cope adequately with common everyday hassles. But then life throws them a curveball. They get sick or need surgery. Someone they love and care for becomes ill, has a stroke, or lands in the hospital. Or their teenage daughters gets pregnant; their married daughter births a severely special-needs baby; their husband retires early from his job; their son divorces his wife; an unexpected house repair or medical expense eats away at family finances. Just when they feel they are handling everything, and think they are doing a fairly good job, change comes along, adds overwhelming stress, and they wonder how in the world they will cope.

The Unsettledness of Change: Change. It comes. And often it deeply disrupts the plans we have made for life. Researcher George Barna writes: "Nothing is exempt from change these days; everything, it seems, is up for grabs, almost every day." He states that current surveys reveal that Americans are the most stressed-out people on earth. Why?

"Largely due to the range and degree of instability and uncertainty we constantly juggle.... There is a high probability that if you lead a normal life (whatever that is), during a single day you will have to negotiate at least one significant emotional, intellectual, moral, spiritual, financial, relational or physical change that has never previously emerged in your life." (39)

Sometimes we can anticipate these "emotional, intellectual, moral, spiritual, financial, relational, and physical" changes that occur. When my friend, Sandy, was told by her two pregnant daughters and one pregnant daughter-in-law that she could expect three little red newborns to come the same spring, Sandy anticipated a dramatic life change. She spent most of winter getting ready for the next year's new deliveries. When they came, she expected them. Anticipated change brings less stress than unexpected change, especially when change comes on top of change. When changes come too closely together, however, they can leave even the most organized woman overwhelmed.

"Not only is change inevitable, occurring at a blistering pace and invading every dimension of our lives, but also the pace of change is accelerating at what seems to be a geometric rate." (40)

We are constantly surrounded by certain stressors—job and otherwise—that can overwhelm us and even break us. It's just part of the fast-paced lifestyles we live.

"It...seems as if our society were designed to break the human spirit," writes Arthur Gish in his book *Beyond the Rat Race*. "Rather than a style of life, it might be called a style of death." (41)

That's frightening. Whether a "style of life" or a "style of death," whether a bear attack or an unexpected crisis, whether expected change or unexpected change, whether stress caused by ourselves or stress caused us by others, we need to constantly maintain a personal health watch and avoid becoming victims of *dis-stress*. Taking time to visit the Quiet Place and spend with God will greatly help us keep our stress levels more normal. Spending quiet time with our Creator will help us better to "trust in the Lord...and in all [our] ways acknowledge him...." (Proverbs 3:5-6 NIV)

Learning the Secrets of Solitude and Silence

Your Personal Time to Reflect and Grow:

- ✓ What is "job stress" and how does it personally affect you? Are you a woman who is highly susceptible to "job stress"? Explain.
- ✓ What did you learn from reading this chapter? How do you plan to use the information?

A Personal Prayer:

Father, help me to trust you more, and to acknowledge you in all things. Keep me coming to the Quiet Place to spend time with you. In Jesus' name, amen.

Chapter 9

Majoring in the Minors

"The lives of the *hurry-sick* lack simplicity."
~ John Ortberg (42)

Not long ago I read about a police rescue in Zephyrhills, Florida. Police Captain Richard Scudder received a frantic phone call. A shopper had spotted a newborn baby left unattended in a locked Dodge Caravan in Wal-Mart's parking lot. It was an unusually hot afternoon, and officer David Feger rushed to the scene. Looking inside, he saw the apparently lifeless infant wrapped in a blanket and strapped into a car seat. The child was not breathing.

Taking immediate action, Feger struggled to open the van door with a "Slim Jim." When that didn't work, he shattered the window with his metal baton. Hoping the child was still alive, he reached inside and touched the unconscious infant.

That's when he discovered that the "unconscious infant" was a plastic doll!

Later the officers had a few laughs. They paid the startled van's owner $243 to fix the broken window. And they got back to work.

We can smile about the incident and agree that the police did the right thing. Too many babies have, indeed, died in sweltering cars in parking lots. But perhaps we can learn something also. Maybe it contains a deeper lesson for society today—a lesson about what happens when we major on the minors in life. (43)

Learning the Secrets of Solitude and Silence

Life Is Too Complicated: Life has become increasingly complicated in the past few decades. Nothing is simple anymore. If we aren't always on guard, we can quickly fill our days with insignificant activities, projects and goals that rescue plastic dolls from locked vans in Wal-Mart parking lots, but don't accomplish any worthwhile purpose. Society has grown so fast-paced that even we Christian women can fail to give ourselves needed time to quietly ponder life, to question our purpose, to seek God's will. For instance, when was the last time we stopped and asked ourselves a major question of faith: "What is the meaning of this short life?"

"Our busy, fast-paced American culture has no time for such a question," writes Thaddeus Barnum. "Our schedules are jam-packed. We don't even have time for ourselves. We're pulled in every direction just to make ends meet."

Barnum is right on target when he writes about today's American busy-ness:

"Today, both parents work full time jobs, and children are left to grow up without their constant presence. For some of us, it's worse. We're faced with the burden of being separated and single. We are left with the mounting guilt of not being present for our kids, stress at work, financial demands, social pressure from friends, and the inner demands—challenging and never ending—to be successful, attractive, pulled together, and in control…. We don't take time to think, dream, read the bible, pray, and wonder about the meaning of life—especially our life." (44)

I meet so many women who allow their days to become super-stressful, who stay far too busy, who hurry too much, and who spend their precious prime-time hours majoring in the minors of life. They don't do it intentionally. It's just that we can get so swept up in the fast-moving current of society that we forget what really is, and what really isn't, important in life. Learning not to major in the minors has been a challenge for me personally. I used to have this crazed notion that mothers could single-handedly solve all the complicated problems faced by each family member. When I finally collapsed from stress and exhaustion, broke a few jaw teeth from nervously grinding them as I slept, and knocked my jaw out of synch, causing incredible pain, I learned something about "majors" and "minors." I finally figured out how many problems I could solve, and what problems I had to let go and be solved by other people. It helped me to slow down into more simplicity and stop hurrying like a hamster on a wheel to get done "all things for all people."

Hurry-Sickness: Meyer Friedman describes frantic life today as "hurry-sickness." I think the name fits. He writes: "Above all [it is] a continuous struggle and unremitting attempt to accomplish or achieve more and more things or participate in more and more events in less and less time, frequently in the face of opposition, real or imagined, from other persons." (45)

Secular culture constantly majors in the minors. It bills as priority the things that should take a rear seat in life.

"Our secular culture tells us that if a person wants to be acceptable she must look good, feel good, and make good," writes author Lewis Smedes.

"The self we are supposed to be comes in a svelte body, draped in designer clothes, and capped with a gorgeous face. Further, she feels fantastic about herself; she feels seductive, alive, adorable, and wholly fulfilled. To top it off, she makes a lot of money and has considerable clout with important people." (46)

These "perfect" size-2 women parade for us across television, iPad and movie screens, smile at us from air-brushed magazine ads, and make us think that clothes, money, beauty, and clout are life's majors to be gained at all costs.

Beauty has become an obsession in our society. Physical attractiveness is highly desired. Some women go to great lengths to achieve and maintain physical beauty because they aren't happy with their bodies. Being unhappy with your body may not seem like a big deal, but experts point out that body dissatisfaction can have far-reaching health consequences.

It's a real public health problem," say Dr. Shari Lusskin, a clinical assistant professor of psychiatry at New York University School of Medicine. "Women who become obsessively preoccupied with their body image can resort to self-destructive means to maintain their body weight at or below their ideal weight." Dr. Lusskin also states that women with body dissatisfaction are more likely to have eating disorders, be depressed, have a lower quality of life, exercise less, and may be less likely to quit smoking, the research found." (47)

The Birthmark: Author Nathaniel Hawthorne addresses this "beauty obsession" in his short story "The Birthmark." The tale begins with Georgiana's scientist husband, Alymer, obsessing about a small flaw on the side of his Barbie-figured, beautiful wife's face. Georgiana's birthmark compels Alymer to mix up a special potion that will rid his wife of this minor flaw. He works frantically in his lab to concoct a remedy; finally successful, he presents her with the draught. She drinks it, and it works—the birthmark fades and disappears. Alymer's triumph turns to despair, though, for soon after the mark is gone, Georgiana is overcome by the poisonous potion and dies. (48) Hawthorne gives us a serious message in this short story.

When the disciples asked Jesus who had the greatest clout and position in God's kingdom, Jesus didn't point to the rich or the beautiful or the prestigious religious leaders of his day. Jesus picked up a little child and put him on his lap. This child is the greatest in the kingdom of heaven, he said (see Matthew 18:1-4).

When a rich, important young man asked Jesus how he could obtain eternal life, Jesus in essence told him to empty his savings account, cash out his high-interest CDs, liquidate his assets, and give all his wealth away (see Matthew 19:16-23). In other words, the rich man majored in the minors [money, possessions, stocks, Calvin Klein], and forgot about the true meaning of life.

When people around Jesus worried about what they would eat or wear, Jesus told them to stop being anxious about food and clothes. They just aren't worth worrying about. A bowl of oatmeal will fill an empty stomach just as quickly as beef roast *au jus.* An outfit from The Salvation Army clearance store will cover your body just as completely as a Liz Claiborne designer suit. Jesus promised that God will supply everything you need (see Matthew 6:25-34).

Forget earth's false treasures, Jesus told his listeners. They are minors. They are plastic baby dolls in locked vans. Concentrate on storing up heaven's treasures—things that won't rust in your garage, things that moths won't eat in your closets, things that won't end up in next spring's garage sale (see Matthew 6:19-24).

These things—clout, clothes, food, money, possessions—aren't major enough to spend your life earning and collecting. Repeatedly Jesus tells us what is really important. Store up heavenly treasures: "For where your treasure is, there your heart will be also" (Matthew 6:21). You can't love both God and money. You have to choose which one to love and which one to hate. God is a major. Money is a minor.

Our Treasure: "Our treasure focuses our heart. 'Your heart will be where your treasure is,' Jesus tells us (Matthew 6:21). Remember that our heart is our will, or our spirit: the center of our being from which our life flows. It is what gives orientation to everything we do. A heart rightly directed therefore brings health and wholeness to the entire personality." (49)

Joseph Girzone writes: "Not that [Jesus] was condemning the possession of things, but the distraction and the craving for them which simulates the worship and attention we should reserve only for God."

Father Girzone warns us, "If we are not careful, craving material things can take the place of our worship of God and cause us to do things that are evil and vile in order to maintain and increase our possessions, even destroying other people in the process."

Jesus gave us his perfect example of how we are to treat Earth's possessions—with a strong sense of detachment.

"Detachment from material possessions was a high priority in Jesus' approach to spirituality, and he exemplified this in his own life." (50)

Do you know women today who are spiritually hungry? They have not found the expected joy and fulfillment in material possessions. They sense an empty place in their lives, a place only God himself can fill. Their souls are dry. Nothing the world offers them seems satisfying.

"Ours is a time of intense spiritual hunger. People are thirsting for the sacred, the mysterious, the mystical. They are looking for more than a good job, a full closet, and a balanced checkbook." (51)

Surely, the pursuit of possessions can quickly waste our days, bring us overwhelming dis-stress, and rob us of our joy.

"When life becomes focused upon God instead of 'things,' one not only is freed from all the anxieties that attend possession, but he also is made free to use 'things' and all the blessing and joy for which they were created and given to us in the first place." (52)

The Necklace: Not long ago I reread Guy de Maupassant's eye-opening story of Matilda, a poor French woman who longed for the world's rich treasures but who had married a good and simple clerk.

"She had neither frocks nor jewels, nothing. And she loved only those things," writes de Maupassant. When her husband, Loisel, brought Matilda a rare and unexpected Cabinet Ball invitation, Matilda cried, "I am vexed not to have a jewel, not one stone, nothing to adorn myself with…. There is nothing more humiliating than to have a shabby air in the midst of rich women!"

Matilda had one well-to-do friend, a former schoolmate at the convent. "Go and find your friend Madame Forestier and ask her to lend you her jewels," Loisel told his wife.

From Mme. Forestier, Matilda borrowed an exquisite necklace of diamonds. Matilda "placed them about her throat…and remained in ecstasy before them."

The day of the ball arrived. Matilda wore the necklace. She

"danced with enthusiasm, with passion, intoxicated with pleasure...." But, after the ball, when Matilda and Loisel arrived home, she discovered to her horror that the necklace was no longer upon her throat. She had lost it. They searched the city for days. They had no money to pay Madame Forestier or to replace it. Finally, in desperation, Matilda and her husband borrowed, at high interest, thirty-six thousand francs. They bought an identical diamond necklace, and Matilda returned it to her friend.

But the heavy debt cost Matilda and Loisel dearly. Matilda took hard scrubwoman jobs and worked without rest for the next ten years. Loisel took on extra tasks at night until they had finally earned enough money to repay the loan with interest. The hard labor and long hours took a toll on the couple. Matilda, once so beautiful and vibrant, now seemed old, "her hair badly dressed, her skirts awry, her hands red...a strong, hard woman...the crude woman of the poor household."

One Sunday, as Matilda took a long overdue walk in the *Champs-Elysees*, she came upon Mme.Forestier, "still young, still pretty, still attractive." Matilda decided to tell her friend about losing the necklace and how she had worked so hard to replace it. Mme. Forestier was shocked.

"You say that you bought a diamond necklace to replace mine?" she asked. Mme. Forestier took Matilda's hands: "Oh, my poor Matilda! Mine were false. They were not worth over five hundred francs!" (53)

Every time I read *The Necklace*, I stop and reexamine my own life, my own wants, my own desires. How often I too have found myself working hard and long hours for the "false necklaces" our culture so craves, the urge to impress that which society so treasures, the empty promises brought by material possessions. Are not all our earthly "treasures" that we work so hard to possess and maintain just worthless fakes in the long run of eternity?

So Much More: God offers us so much more. He gives us eternal treasures, riches that will last. How quickly we can get caught up in the rat race to acquire what society values. How easily we settle for less than what God offers us. God offers us true treasure—communion with him, solitude and sacred silence.

Coming to Christ in the Quiet Place is not for the purpose of recharging our batteries in order to "enter life's many competitions with new vigor and strength." Although it often does that very thing. When we emerge from the Quiet Place, "we find that solitude gives us power not to win the rat race but to ignore the rat race altogether." (54) The rat race is no longer attractive to us. We've tasted a much deeper, more fulfilling happiness than society can ever offer us.

It's true. Coming to the Quiet Place increases our desire to give up those things that have no eternal value and to reclaim those things that have true and lasting value. It is in the Quiet Place that God whispers to us and makes us aware of life's true treasure—himself. In relationship with the living Christ, frocks and jewels entice us no longer. We realize earth's diamond necklaces hold little value to us. We regard possessions as tools to be used, not loved and adored, labored for and stored. "Get all you *can*, *can* all you get, and then sit on the *can*" is no longer our motto. In the Quiet Place, God helps us discover the place of possessions in our earthly lives. He helps us to drastically shift our priorities from the world to him—to close our eyes at what the world values and to really see the gifts he offers. In the Quiet Place, God offers us the freedom of simplicity from our possessions. Simplicity is simply "a lessened evaluation of what the world promotes as important." (55)

As I reread the gospels, I discover that Jesus did all the work his Father gave him to do without becoming overwhelmed and dis-stressed. In the beautiful prayer he prayed shortly before his death, Jesus said to his Father: "I have brought you glory on earth by completing the work you gave me to do" (John 17:4). How I long for those to be my final words as I depart this life— "I have completed the work you gave me to do!" If I can't see myself saying this, perhaps it is because I am far too busy with work that God doesn't intend for me to do—unimportant work, majoring-in-the-minors work! Perhaps I don't have my priorities in God's order.

Jesus did his work with love and compassion, showing no irritation when people interrupted him. Was it because Jesus spent considerable time in the Quiet Place with God, and that, through prayer, he came to understand his priorities? Was it that those things so important to our society—clothes, food, homes, possessions—held no interest for Jesus? Jesus wanted only to do his Father's will. He didn't desire to possess or impress. He held on to nothing except his intense love for God and his compassionate service-love for people. He didn't make New Year's resolutions. His main purpose was to praise and glorify God and to complete the work God gave him to do. He lived a balanced life, even though he worked hard and at times hurt with hunger and exhaustion. Jesus' life wasn't easy, but he didn't spend precious time searching for his "sense of self" or for "personal fulfillment" and "happiness." These came as by-products of his intimate relationship with his Father in the Quiet Place.

Jesus' Priorities: Jesus clearly knew what his priorities were, for he spent a large portion of his day in communication with God in the Quiet Place. It is in the Quiet Place with the Father that we can slow down, rethink our priorities, diminish our stress, reevaluate our treasures, and decide what is really valuable in life.

No doubt you hear, as I do, the cry of Christian women all over the country, women who are "thirsting for the sacred, the mysterious, the mystical." Women who are, indeed, "looking for more than a good job, a full closet, and a balanced checkbook." They are tired of the lifestyle that stresses their bodies and holds little value or meaning to their souls. As our society becomes more and more complicated, intense, and hurried, we will probably hear more cries from weary women—women who are fed up with frantic paces and fruitless pursuits. Women who yearn to spend time in the Quiet Place.

Let's listen carefully to their longings. Let's point them to the Quiet Place and to the One who waits there with outstretched arms.

Your Personal Time to Reflect and Grow:

- ✓ Ponder this statement and decide what it means to you: "Ours is a time of intense spiritual hunger. People are thirsting for the sacred, the mysterious, the mystical. They are looking for more than a good job, a full closet, and a balanced checkbook." Do you agree? Why or why not?
- ✓ Stop and ask yourself this question: "What is the meaning of this short life?" Write down your answer.

A Personal Prayer:

Father, help me to know the difference in life's priorities—those things I do that are eternal and those things I do that are only temporary and of no lasting value. Show me how to spend my brief life doing the things that count for eternity. I pray these things in Jesus' name, amen.

Chapter 10

De-Stressing and Resting Our Body

"I went to the woods because I wished to live deliberately, to confront only the essential facts of life, and see if I could not learn what it had to teach, and not, when I came to die, discover that I had not lived."
~ **Henry David Thoreau, 1845 (56)**

We've already discussed how today's Christian woman usually works too hard, bears too many responsibilities, deals with far too much stress, and allows herself little, if any, personal time to relax. Many women race through their days at breakneck speed to work outside jobs; run an efficient household, love, support, and encourage a busy husband; and rear happy healthy children, keeping them all safe, sheltered, fed, dressed, educated, and churched. All the while, society tells women to work harder, accomplish more, and rest less.

Consider Your Work Outside the Home: "Come to me, all you who labor," Jesus said. "Labor" means to perform work under wearisome or grievous circumstances; to toil with difficulty, to exert, to strive, to take pains, to travail. Those of us who work outside the home can relate to "labor" and its meaning. As mentioned earlier, while some women can make choices about whether or not to work outside the home, many women cannot. For various reasons, they must work, and they must work hard, long hours in order to support themselves and their families. Most of the time these are single women, especially single moms who support themselves and their children with a sole income. Some women choose to work because they enjoy having extra money to buy those things that one salary can't afford. Usually these women are married, with or without children, and donate their salaries to the household's budget. Some women work because their husbands can't work or won't work, or because their husbands ask them or expect them to work outside the home. Whatever the reason a woman embraces employment, the following practical issues are important to consider:

- ❖ What are the reasons I am working outside my home?
- ❖ Am I fulfilling someone else's expectations for me through my work?
- ❖ Do I need the money? What do I need the money for?
- ❖ Am I wise in the ways I spend the money I work hard for?
- ❖ Could I simplify my life (and/or my family's life) and choose not to work outside my home? Could we get by financially?
- ❖ Am I working physically harder than I want to work, or should work?
- ❖ Have I somehow confused my self-worth with the type of work I do?
- ❖ Does this job give me my self-esteem, or am I able to draw my self-esteem solely from God?
- ❖ Am I working so hard that I am hurting my physical health?
- ❖ Is the extra income worth the extra physical toil and risks to my health?
- ❖ Is my marriage suffering because of my job?
- ❖ Are my children suffering because of my job?
- ❖ Is my personal time with God suffering because of my job?
- ❖ Do I yearn to spend more time with God and family, but

don't have time because of employment?
- ❖ What am I teaching my children about work, money, and their values?
- ❖ If I had a choice whether or not to work outside the home, which would I choose?

When we stop to look at our work habits and schedules, and truly consider their advantages and disadvantages, we can better make those decisions about our outside employment. If you must work outside your home, decide on ways to make your work more meaningful and less physically exerting. For instance:

- ❖ Do you feel "God-called" to this particular vocation or work?
- ❖ Are you working within God's plan for your life? Have you seriously prayed about your vocation in light of God's purpose for you?
- ❖ Are you doing the kind of work you enjoy, are trained to do, and find satisfying?
- ❖ Are you working because you love your job and the contributions you make to your family and community?
- ❖ Do you find your job an important outlet for your creativity?
- ❖ Would you find work elsewhere to be more fulfilling and less irritating?
- ❖ Are you taking on more responsibility than your job should require?
- ❖ Can you negotiate fewer demands and responsibilities on the job?
- ❖ Can you lessen your commute time to and from work? Or take public transportation? Or carpool?
- ❖ Can you rearrange your work hours to better benefit your and your family's schedule?
- ❖ Can you negotiate more vacation time, sick days, rest days?
- ❖ Could you use your lunch hour as a rest time? Is a quiet place available in your workplace to allow you to enjoy

some quiet time.
- ❖ Financially, could you afford to work a part time instead of full time job?
- ❖ If you must work, can you afford to hire some help with the housework and childcare so you can find more time to rest?
- ❖ Are you spending more time than is necessary doing jobs that might require fewer hours?
- ❖ Are you "working smart" and thereby saving valuable time?

Once again, women who work hard, both outside and inside their homes, need adequate sleep and quiet personal time. Otherwise, they do harm to their physical bodies. God created our bodies to need regular rest and renewal, if even for a short period of time.

"There is great value in even a brief respite," writes Albert Meiburg. "If Jesus felt it necessary to go into a quiet place to recover his strength, how much more do we? Your quiet place may be a weekend getaway with your spouse. A new scene may give you stimulation and time to get back in touch with each other." (57)

More and more women in today's workforce are questioning the reasons they work outside the home. They are working smarter and, thus, learning to accomplish more in a shorter period of time. They are simplifying their lives, selling the mansions with the unmanageable mortgages, driving less expensive cars for longer periods of time, shopping less for clothes, living with fewer luxuries, and teaching their children to want less of society's cleverly advertised merchandise.

Smart women today are putting their priorities in order. They are spending more quiet time with God in prayer, Bible study, devotional reading, family and congregational worship times. They are allowing their tired bodies to seek silence and solitude. They are coming more often to the Quiet Place, and they are staying there longer.

Women today are questioning the things society holds so

dear. They are figuring out what life's true values are. Many are choosing to retreat into simple lifestyles, those ways of living that leave them time for the things they truly treasure. They are turning their backs on the ideals promoted by retailers and Hollywood. They are yearning for a new simplicity, a "Walden Pond" type of life.

Walden Pond: In 1845, Henry David Thoreau took inventory of his life and decided to turn his back on the hustle and bustle of Concord, Massachusetts. He built a simple cabin in the woods near Walden Pond, and in his book *Walden*, he records his eye-opening experiences of solitude and silence, urging his readers to simplify their lives. He writes:

"I did not wish to live what was no life, living is so dear, or did I wish to practice resignation, unless it was quite necessary. I wanted to live deep and suck out all the marrow of life, to live so sturdily and Spartan-like as to put to rout all that was not life." (58).

Thoreau lived near Walden Pond for two years, two months, and two days, concentrating on what he called the essential facts of life. At the end of his sojourn there, with sensitive insight from his experience, he asks, "Why should we live with such hurry and waste of life?" (59)

Perhaps Thoreau's question should be our question, too.

Your Personal Time to Reflect and Grow:

- ✓ Why should we, as Christian women, take the time to think through our priorities?
- ✓ -What does it mean to simplify life? In what ways have you yourself done this? What were the results of this action?

A Personal Prayer:

Father, show me the plan you have for my life. Meet me in the Quiet Place and teach me all those things I need to learn. In Jesus' name, amen.

Chapter 11

Transforming Our Body

"Man cannot long survive without air, water, and sleep. Next in importance comes food. And close on its heels, solitude." ~ Thomas Szasz (60)

Seek solitude and silence. Treasure them. Protect them. Our times of solitude and silence help replenish our tired bodies, relieve our everyday stress, give us time to breathe deeply, to think, to ponder life, and to rest our souls. Silence and solitude can energize us so that we can return to our workloads with greater physical strength and endurance. They also help us decide which workloads are worth returning to—which majors to keep and which minors to discard.

Scripture tells us our physical body is a temple of God's Holy Spirit. God designed our bodies to function well and to serve him, others, and ourselves. Let us accept his gift of a physical body with gratefulness. Let us doubly thank him if our bodies are strong and healthy. The human body is a miracle! Let us take good care of it.

"Be altruistic but take care of yourself at the same time. If you are going to serve others well, you must at the same time survive and do well yourself. Let us consider Nature's model as we think about our bodies. All the tissues in your body are altruistic except cancer cells. Cooperate with your own tissues. The *joie de vivre*, or joy of life, has an enormous preventive and healing effect." (61)

Rest Your Body: Your body needs the tender loving care that rest brings to it. Human bodies aren't machines. They cannot work and produce without regular periods of total rest. They require time to replenish themselves. God created our body to need physical rest.

Your Personal Time to Reflect and Grow:

- ✓ How do you rest your body? What do these times of rest mean to you?
- ✓ Why is solitude and silence so important to the body's rest? Why should we treasure those times and protect them? What happens to our body when we don't rest it?

A Personal Prayer:

Father, thank you for the gift of a body. Teach me how to take care of it so that I can continue to serve you in ministry. In Jesus' name, amen.

Section 3

Healing
the Spirit

"Come to me, all you who are heavy laden
and I will give you rest."
~ Matthew 11:28 NKJV

Chapter 12

Yoked with Heavy Burdens

"Love the Lord with all your heart." ~ Matthew 22:37

Jesus invites all of us who are "heavy laden" or "soul burdened" or "heart burdened" to come to him. *Soul* (or *spirit*) "is a cipher for our spiritual attributes, like being courageous or timid. *Heart* is the most important term in [Scripture] for referring to the inner nature." For instance, Jesus tells us to "love the Lord your God with all your *heart*" (Matthew 22:37). This means "we are to love God with every fiber of our being." (62)

I am discovering that, in some ways, all women are "heavy laden" and somewhat "soul burdened." Some of us wear heavy yokes placed on us by other people, people who have unrealistic expectations for us, people who expect us to handle their emergencies, people who believe we must do their work. Others of us wear heavy yokes placed on us by society, bosses, co-workers, in-laws, and even circumstances. Some of us wear heavy yokes that we, for whatever reason, place on our own necks.

Maybe you carry in your heart a heavy burden. Perhaps your soul is heavy laden and weary. If so, I have an answer for you, no matter how heavy your burden, no matter how laden your soul. His name is Jesus. He loves you perfectly. And he waits, right now, for you to join him in the Quiet Place. There you can talk and cry and commune with him in sacred solitude. There you can place your head on his strong shoulder and find rest for your heart and soul. Jesus invites you to take his yoke upon you and learn from him. He promises that his yoke is easy to wear and his burden is light.

The Yoke: Jesus chose a perfect and beautiful example when he used the image of the yoke. In ancient days in the Middle East, Egypt, and other lands, a farmer chose two hardworking, muscular animals, usually oxen, to plow his field. If you've ever walked through the Holy Land, you know the fields require strong beasts to pull the plows. The ground, sunbaked and hard as brick, is covered with large and small rocks.

Yokes were heavy wooden harnesses that kept two animals walking side by side. Placed upon the animals' necks, the yoke ensured that each ox pulled in relatively equal strength in order to plow the hard ground. They shared the heavy burden. As the animals struggled to pull the attached plow, the rough wood of the yoke scraped and tore at their shoulders and necks. The yokes were so heavy the animals oftentimes couldn't bend their necks.

Ancient Middle-Eastern oxen knew all about carrying heavy burdens—it was their life work. Sometimes the farmer raised or bought an untrained plow animal. In order to teach the younger, weaker animal to wear the yoke and plow the field, the farmer yoked him to a muscular, experienced ox. The strong, well-trained ox bore the bulk of the yoke while the newer animal learned how to plow. While the yoke on the experienced animal proved doubly heavy, the animal trainee's yoke was light and easy.

When Jesus uses this yoke example, he offers us, the weaker trainee, to share the yoke with him, the experienced muscular one. We walk beside him, work with him, and learn from him, but he takes the burdens and carries them for us. He pulls the plow. He offers us his divine rest from our heavy burdens (see Matthew 11:29-30 NKJV).

Matthew Henry calls the yoke Jesus offers us "a yoke...lined with love" and "a yoke of pleasantness." Henry said that we need not fear his yoke. "His commandments are holy, just, and good. It requires self-denial, and exposes us to difficulties, but this is abundantly repaid, even in this world, by inward peace and joy." (63)

It is in the Quiet Place that we hear Jesus' offer to carry our heart's burdens. It is in solitude and silence that we can offer him our laden soul and enter into rest. Why do you and I so often lug our heavy hearts and weary souls all by ourselves when Jesus waits to help us carry the bulk of the load?

"Jesus promises that his yoke will be kind and gentle to our shoulders, enabling us to carry our load more easily. That is what he means when he says his burden is 'light.' Actually, it might be quite heavy, but we will be able to carry it. Why? Because Jesus himself will help us. It is as though he tells us, 'Walk alongside me; learn to carry the burden by observing how I do it. If you let me help you, the heavy labor will seem lighter.'" (64)

What burdens your heart today? What keeps your soul heavy laden? Is it fear? Or guilt? Or depression? Or worry? Or hate? Or bitterness? Or selfishness? Or deceit? Or pride? Or lust? Or sadness? Or despair?

The list could go on almost indefinitely. Women today, around the world, are burdened by many things. The more I travel, the more I realize that most of the problems women face are universal. As I've talked with women in Japan and England and Europe and the Middle East, as well as other places around the globe, I have been amazed to discover how closely their individual problems resemble the current struggles of American women. They too deal with such things as fear of job loss, heavy work stress, financial difficulties, marital conflict, divorce, abandonment, spousal abuse, parenting and grand parenting problems, deaths of loved ones, a loved one's suicide, personal illness, serious surgery, caring for ill or elderly parents, depression, natural disasters, war, terrorism, and the list goes on.

As he did throughout the gospels, Jesus opens his arms to those who worry about life's basic needs—food and clothes—and says, "Don't worry about tomorrow—about your food or clothes, for your heavenly Father knows that you need them. Just come to me...trust me, I am your provider...bring me your worries, your burdens...I will give you rest" (see Matthew 6:25-34). "Here," he says, "slip this yoke over your shoulders. I'll bear the heavy burden for you; I'll take the weight of the yoke and pull the plow. Your part of the work will be light and easy. I can pull the load for both of us."

What are the emotional weights that burden our hearts and keep our souls from coming to the Quiet Place where God waits for us? Why do we choose to remain heavy laden with worries and concerns and frustrations and fears when Jesus offers us rest?

Your Personal Time to Reflect and Grow:

- ✓ Describe what Scripture means by heavy laden and burdened.
- ✓ What are the heavy burdens you now carry?

A Personal Prayer:

Father, please help me carry my heavy burdens. I bring you my worries, and I trust you to provide me with rest. In Jesus' name, amen.

Chapter 13

Guarding Our Heart to Actively Love

> "If I speak with human eloquence and angelic ecstasy but don't have love, I'm nothing but the creaking of a rusty gate...." ~ from 1 Corinthians 13, *The Message*

We cannot always control the things that happen to us: unexpected illnesses, deaths, or divorces that grip our heart and break it into small pieces. Pain caused by circumstances can leave us hurting. Suffering the offenses caused by others can drive our souls into deep despair. A woman can react in one of two ways when she faces suffering caused by circumstances or by those she has trusted: (1) She can allow the pain to draw her closer to God. She can answer his call, "Come to me...and find rest." (2) Or she can allow her suffering to make her bitter, to drive a wedge between herself and her heavenly Father. When she allows her sorrows to separate her from the One who truly loves her, the One who asks to wear her yoke, then she is doubly hurt. She causes herself even more pain, pain she doesn't need to suffer.

God Made Your Heart to Love: Always choose love in your life...love for God and love for others. Whenever you face hate, combat it with a heart filled with love. Hate is a cancer that attacks and heart and eats our soul. Hate "cells" attach themselves to healthy "cells" and multiply. They can quickly spread and take over a person's life and render it useless for God's kingdom work. You and I need no explanation of hate. We see the destructive enemy each morning when we read the daily news. We see hate in road rage and murder and terrorism. The only antidote to hate is love—unconditional and illogical love.

What Is Love?: American women, even devoted Christian women, are often confused about love's real meaning. Movies, magazines, and society in general have taught us falsehoods. Hollywood's version of love has nothing to do with Scripture's version. What society believes is true love is instead true lust. The sweaty hands, the thumping heart, the butterfly stomach—those prove to be awesome (wonderful and terrible) feelings, but they are just feelings, not fact. While lust feelings soon evaporate, genuine love grows deeper with each passing day.

Genuine love is not a *feeling* at all. Real love is something we *do*—love is a verb. Feelings have little to do with the love Scripture so beautifully defines.

In the English language, we have one word for *love*, and it is *love*. We use the same word to describe our affection for our mother as for our enjoyment of strawberry ice cream. We love God, and we love our children. We love our country, and we love our country club. We love to fish, and we love to eat out with our spouse. Our one word *love* makes no distinction between degrees of affection or strength of conviction. The context of our statement must awkwardly hint at the type of love we mean.

Biblical Love Versus Societal Love: People in Jesus' day had several separate and distinctive words for "love." No one had to stop and guess what another meant when he used the most beautiful biblical word for love: *agape*. Agape is that perfect, selfless, unconditional, I-love-you-no-matter-what-you-do God-love. Agape love is how God loves you and me in Jesus Christ. It's a perfect verb-love. It continues to love even when we fail to feel it. It remains solid even when our feelings shift, even when we are uncertain or unaware of it.

Are you and I capable of loving with agape? I'm not sure we can ever reach that high on the love scale. But that's the love Jesus calls us to strive to reach. Agape is the love that allows us to love those who hate us and those who hurt us. Agape is the love that keeps us showing love to the trusted friend who betrays us, to the unloving husband who abandons us, to the irresponsible mother who deserts us, to the disgraceful father who abuses us, to the wily church member who takes advantage of us, to the lust-filled employer who harasses us. Only agape can accomplish these feats, for it is supernatural love. Agape is God's love—unconditional, persevering, purposeful, and perfect. We find this Scriptural agape love in 1 Corinthians 13, as we read Paul's beautiful words.

Jesus talked about agape love:
"You have heard that it was said, 'Love your neighbor and hate your enemy.' But I tell you: Love your enemies and pray for those who persecute you, that you may be sons of your Father in heaven…. If you love those who love you, what reward will you get? Are not even the tax collectors doing that? And if you greet only your brothers, what are you doing more than others? Do not even pagans do that? Be perfect, therefore, as your heavenly Father is perfect. (Matthew 5:43-48).

"Praying for his or her enemies distinguishes the Christian from everyone else. It is appropriate behavior for followers of Jesus. Praying for an enemy…gives something back for the coming generation because it helps break the cycle of hate and fear. It's tough! But it's necessary." (65)

Verb-love is selfless. It always puts others first. It reaches out and loves even the unlovely. According to Paul, verb-love "never gives up" but "keeps going to the end." According to Jesus, verb-love even "loves enemies" and "prays for those who persecute you." Verb-love loves the rebellious teenager who selfishly holds out his hand for more money and cares nothing for the future of his family. Oh, how richly Shakespeare captured this ungrateful prodigal: "Sharper than a serpent's tooth is the thankless child!" But the loving Father loves even the unlovely boy. He waits by the window and looks far into the distance watching for the familiar gait of his beloved son. When the loving Father sees the repentant son, he runs out to meet him—this boy who smells of sweat and swine. He welcomes him back into the family and throws a party to celebrate his return. (See the "Prodigal Son" story in Luke 15:11-32).

Jesus used this story to show the Father's unconditional verb-love. Love is not a feeling but an action. We can love our enemies because love is not something we feel but something we choose to do. Love is a kindness extended to someone who doesn't deserve that kindness. Genuine love—Christ's agape—can motivate us to do things for others that we would never consider doing otherwise.

This is love beyond human affection. When we love others, especially the "unlovely," we move beyond mere human love. We love them with God's love. God's love allows us to see the world with his eyes, to love humanity with his heart, and to reach out with his hands to those who hurt. That's agape, divine gift-love.

Verb-love is love in action, even when no one knows it. The greatest account of verb-love is John 3:16: "For God so loved the world that He gave His only begotten Son, that whoever believes in Him should not perish but have everlasting life." God had this kind of love for you and me when he willingly gave his only Son to die on the cross.

Little Tree: One of the most meaningful stories about verb-love is the one about Little Tree. Little Tree is a poor young Cherokee boy who lives with his grandparents in the Tennessee mountains in the 1930s. One day, as he stretches out on the creek bank, hand-fishing in a mountain stream—just the way his Native-American "Granpa" had taught him—the small boy hears a "dry rustle that started slow and got faster until it made a whirring noise."

"I turned my head toward the sound," remembers Little Tree. "It was a rattlesnake. He was coiled to strike, his head in the air, and looking down on me, not six inches from my face."

Little Tree "froze sill and couldn't move."

"He was bigger around than my leg and I could see ripples moving under his dry skins," he recalls. "He was mad. Me and the snake stared at each other. He was flicking out his tongue—nearly in my face—and his eyes was slitted—red and mean."

While the snake decides which part of Little Tree's face to strike, a shadow falls gently over them. It was Granpa.

"Don't turn yer head. Don't move, Little Tree," he says. "Don't even blink yer eyes."

As the snake raises his head and prepares to attack Little Tree, Granpa's big hand slips between the boy's face and the snake's fangs.

"The hand stayed steady as a rock...the rattler struck, fast and hard. He hit Granpa's hand like a bullet.... I saw the needle fangs bury up in the meat as the rattler's jaws took up half his hand."

A loving grandfather takes a snake's stinging bite—a bite meant for his grandson. Then, "Granpa...grabbed the rattler behind the head, and he squeezed.... Granpa...choked that snake to death with one hand, until I heard the crack of backbone. Then he threw him on the ground."

Granpa almost died from that snakebite. He took that snake's bite to save Little Tree from a painful death. That's verb-love. (66)

Guard your heart against all those bitter weeds that can cause hate to enter into it. Guard it and keep it to show God's self giving verb-love to others.

Your Personal Time to Reflect and Grow:

- ✓ What did you find meaningful about the story of Little Tree?
- ✓ What is your own definition of verb-love?

A Personal Prayer:

Father, please guard my heart against anything that might render it unable to show your love, verb-love to others. In Jesus' name, amen.

Chapter 14

Finding Nurture and Nourishment

> **"I am doing now what I will do for all eternity. I am blessing God, praising Him, adoring Him, and loving Him with all my heart." ~ Brother Lawrence**

One of my spiritual mentors is Brother Lawrence, a monk born in 1611, who spent his life working in the monastery's kitchen in Paris. In the midst of steaming pots, noisy pans, and clanging dishes, Brother Lawrence practiced the presence of God. No matter how noisy the kitchen became or how many monks passed through and interrupted his private worship, Brother Lawrence communed without ceasing with the Lord he so loved. Somehow Brother Lawrence "learned to cultivate the deep presence of God so thoroughly in his own heart that he was able to joyfully exclaim, 'I am doing now what I will do for all eternity. I am blessing God, praising Him, adoring Him, and loving Him with all my heart.' …It is God who paints Himself in the depths of our souls. We must merely open our hearts to receive Him and His loving presence." (67)

This monk loved peace and quiet and solitude, yet for some reason God placed him in the busy and noisy and chaotic monastery kitchen. What did he do? He found the Quiet Place within his own heart and soul, and there he continually communed with God. His heart became his chapel, and he lived there deep within the Quiet.

Perhaps you, like me, long for silence and solitude, yet find yourself surrounded by interruptions, requests, emergencies, and general restless noise. How many times I have longed for that quiet mountainside lodge where I could lose myself in the sacred silence of the Quiet Place. But we can't stay in the lodge forever. For we are involved from head to toe in the busyness of life in today's harried society. How can you and I, in the clang and clamor of an ordinary day, guard our heart and allow God to nurture our soul? Here are some practical suggestions:

- ❖ **Make Your Heart a Chapel**
  We don't have to be sitting or kneeling in church in order to pray. God lives only a whisper away. We can come to his Quiet Place within our own hearts and commune with him there. Brother Lawrence reminds us, "It isn't necessary that we stay in church in order to remain in God's presence. We can make our heart a chapel where we can go anytime to talk to God privately." (68)

  And there, in your private chapel, get to know God. Brother Lawrence said, "We have to know someone before we can truly love them. In order to know God, we must think about Him often. And once we get to know Him, we will think about Him even more often, because where our treasure is, there also is our heart." (69)

- ❖ **Meditate on God's Word**
  We can find the answers to our faith-questions within the pages of Scripture. Allow God's Word to be your guidebook for life, for it is a miracle book, inspired by God himself.

  Imagine the divine dynamics God designed to give us his Word between the covers of one book! The word Bible means "books" or "scrolls."

- **How should we approach the Bible?**
  1. As the inspired Word of God (2 Timothy 3:6; Hebrews 1:1);
  2. As the inspired Word of the Holy Spirit (2 Peter 1:21; Acts 1:16);
  3. As the sacred book that presents Christ.

- **How do we find understanding as to the meaning of Scripture?**
  1. Through the work of the Holy Spirit (1 Corinthians 2:14-15; Psalm 119:18).

- **Why must we trust Scripture?**
  1. Because it is a gift from God to us;
  2. Jesus trusted the Scriptures as God's authoritative Word (Matthew 19:4; 22:29);
  3. Paul and the apostles believed the scrolls to be the "very words of God" (Romans 3:2).

- **How have believers considered God's Word in the past?**
  1. As the "Word of Christ";
  2. As the "Word of Life";
  3. As the "Word of Truth";
  4. As a two-edged sword that is not to be added to or taken from;
  5. Not to be handled deceitfully;
  6. To be searched and studied and taught;
  7. To be read publicly.

  The Westminster Confession of 1646 says: "The authority of the Holy Scripture, for which it ought to be believed and obeyed, depends not upon the testimony of any man or church, but wholly upon God (who is truth), the Author thereof; and therefore it is to be received, because it is the Word of God."

- **What does Scripture tell us about itself?**
1. "All Scripture is God-breathed and is useful for teaching, rebuking, correcting and training in righteousness, so that the man of God may be thoroughly equipped for every good work" (2 Timothy 3:16-17);
2. "The unfolding of your words gives light; it gives understanding to the simple" (Psalm 119:130);
3. "Heaven and earth will pass away, but my words will never pass away" (Matthew 24:35);
4. "Your Word is a lamp to my feet and a light for my path" (Psalm 119:105);
5. "The Word became flesh and made his dwelling among us. We have seen his glory, the glory of the One and Only, who came from the Father, full of grace and truth" (John 1:14).

- **What are we supposed to do with God's Word?**
1. "Do your best to present yourself to God as one approved, a workman who does not need to be ashamed and who correctly handles the word of truth" (2 Timothy 2:15);
2. "Let the word of Christ dwell in you richly as you teach and admonish one another with all wisdom" (Colossians 3:15);
3. "If you remain in me and my words remain in you, ask whatever you wish, and it will be given you. This is to my Father's glory, that you bear much fruit, showing yourselves to be my disciples" (John 15:7-8);
4. "I have hidden your Word in my heart that I might not sin against you" (Psalm 119:11).

Dr. W. A. Criswell, in his book *Why I Preach That the Bible Is Literally True*, writes that the Bible is the literal, inspired, God-breathed truth of heaven, the book that reveals to us truth that is able to bring us into living union with God. Jesus read and quoted the

Bible as verbally inspired.

Imagine how the Bible came into being! The Bible contains sixty-six books written by forty different men. It was written on two continents, in countries hundreds of miles apart. The Bible was written in deserts, wildernesses, caves, tents, prisons, and palaces. It was written in three different languages (Hebrew, Aramaic, and Greek). The first part of the Bible was written 1500 years before the last part was written. It took sixteen centuries to write the Bible!

It was written by people of every level of political and social life—from a king on his throne to a shepherd in his field to a fisherman on the sea. It was written both by educated princes and poets and philosophers and physicians to fishermen and tax collectors. Yet Dr. Criswell acknowledges the Bible is one complete organic unity and whole. Every part of the Bible fits every other part. There is one ever-increasing, ever-growing, ever-developing plan pervading the whole. It contains one system of doctrine, one system of ethics, one plan of salvation, and one rule of faith. There is a perfect harmony throughout the Scriptures from the first verse in Genesis to the last verse in Revelation. It is a masterminded book! A living book! It has challenged people for thousands of years—even though entire civilizations and governments have tried to destroy it. It is still the number-one bestseller! (70)

I greatly miss W. A. Criswell since his death. I've enjoyed many wonderful conversations with this great preacher over the years. When we spoke, he called me "daughter." I liked that. His genuine love for God's Word proved contagious.

God's Word, the Bible, is a living book—a personal, intimate letter from God to you and me (Hebrews 4:12). Let us make a place and a time each day to read, study, and reflect upon God's Word.

❖ Seek Silent Places

I often seek out quiet places where I can meditate and pray without interruption or schedule. I find that silence nurtures my soul. I come back to my busy world refreshed after I sip Jesus' living water. The quiet has a calming effect on my soul.

Mother Teresa was right when she said, "We cannot put ourselves directly in the presence of God if we do not practice internal and external silence.... Silence gives us a new outlook on everything...." The compassionate nun suggested that we "listen in silence because if your heart is full of other things you cannot hear the voice of God." (71)

Even though you and I must sometimes search for silence, let us diligently seek it with all our heart.

"Solitude seeks to silence a noisy world. But it is also a tool to quiet our souls, which are often wracked by their own inner turmoil, tensions, and troubles." (72)

Visit your place of sacred solitude often, for it is "a place where your mind can be idle, and forget its concerns, descend into silence, and worship the Father in secret. There can be no contemplation where there is no secret." (73)

How God yearns for us to slow down, to "Be still, and know that [He is] God" (Psalm 46:10).

Your Personal Time to Reflect and Grow:

- ✓ Do you have a place of solitude and silence that you can meet with God? Why is this important to you and to your faith?
- ✓ What does Scripture mean to you when the psalmist tells us to "Be still, and know that [He is] God"?

Learning the Secrets of Solitude and Silence

A Personal Prayer:

Father, help me to seek out silent places where I can meet with you, pray, converse, and commune in solitude. The world is such a busy place. Create within my heart a quiet chapel so that I may visit it even in the noise of society all around me. In Jesus' name, I pray, amen.

Chapter 15

The Transformation of Our Soul

"Come to Me, all you who labor and are heavy laden, and I will give you rest. Take my yoke upon you and learn from me, for I am gentle and humble in heart, and you will find rest for your souls. For my yoke is easy and my burden is light." ~ Matthew 11:28, 29-30 NKJV

Jesus waits by our side, ever-present to transform our mind, our body, our heart, and our soul with his divine gift of presence.

- ❖ **Come to him in solitude.** Solitude means "being out of human contact, being alone, and being so for lengthy periods of time." (74)
- ❖ **Come to him in silence.** "Silence means to escape from sounds, noises, other than the gentle ones of nature." (75)
- ❖ **Come to him in quiet prayer.** "In the silence of the heart God speaks. If you face God in prayer and silence, God will speak to you.... Souls of prayer are souls of great silence." (76)
- ❖ **Come to him in repentance.** As we gradually gain more insight into ourselves, we are able, with God's grace, to find ways to resist habitual sin and grow in self-control. We gain strength bit by bit, like an athlete striving for the prize. Gradually we reclaim more and more of ourselves and offer it to God's transforming light. Thus the Holy Spirit works within us, sanctifying us from the inside out. (77)

- **Come to him with mind, body, and spirit.** We are not only mind (thought and emotions) and body, but we are also spirit. Our spirit is the part of our being that resonates with beauty, shows compassion to the wounded, avoids evil, and reaches upward for a relationship with the Creator. Through our personal spirit God the Father teaches us, communicates with us.... When our personal spirit is nurtured through communion with God, worship, and exposure to beauty our whole being flourishes. (78)
- **Come to him in honesty.** Human withdrawal is a very painful and lonely process, because it forces us to face directly our own condition in all its beauty as well as misery. When we are not afraid to enter into our own center and to concentrate on the stirrings of our own soul, we come to know that being alive means being loved. (79)
- **Come to him in humility.** Humility is not the same as resisting the urge to show off (which is modesty) or denying that you have gifts and talents (which is lying). Humility is remembering that you have a beam in your eye. In every situation remember what God knows about you, and how much you have been forgiven.... Account yourself the "chief of sinners" and be gracious toward the failings of others. (80)
- **Come to Him and seek his face.** Do you have a place of shelter where you seek only his face? Do you spend time in that secret place? Have you given prayer the priority it deserves? When you pray, remember it is the Lord's face you seek. (81)
- **Come to him for peace.** God offers us divine peace. Divine peace is a deep inner confidence in God. In fact, it is possible to have the peace of God even in the midst of war. Divine peace is not dependent on outside circumstances. It can flourish even when external circumstances are absolutely the worst they can be. (82)

❖ **Come to him for transformation.** "If we mature spiritually, we also will be increasingly transformed into Christ's image" (Romans 8:29). (83)

Dear sister in Christ, come to the Quiet Place, for it is there that Jesus waits for you and offers you his deep communion. Come to the Quiet, for it is there that Jesus teaches you the secrets of solitude and silence and peace.

I treasure this time I've spent with you. Thank you for journeying with me throughout the pages of this book. I hope God's Word, written within these chapters, has blessed you and encouraged you. Life is not easy. But Jesus shares your yoke.

As I write these final words, my prayer for you is this:
The Lord bless you and keep you;
The Lord make his face shine upon you
And be gracious to you.
The Lord turn his face toward you
And give you peace. (Numbers 6:24-26)

A note from the author:

I pray that this book has helped you in some way. If it has, would you please let me know? Please email me at cdwg@aol.com and tell me how these words have ministered to you. And if you would write a brief review, post it on Amazon.com under this book title (and/or Goodreads.com, and/or BarnesandNoble.com) perhaps you will encourage other hurting women to read this book and find help. Thank you and may God richly bless you!

~ Denise George

About the Author

Denise George has been writing and publishing for 35 years. She has authored 25 books, and has published more than 1500 articles for magazines such as *Redbook*, *Essence*, *Guideposts*, *Decision*, and many others. She teaches "The Writing Minister" (writing-to-publish) course for seminarians at Beeson Divinity School, Samford University, Birmingham, AL. Her latest book is *While the World Watched* (Carolyn McKinstry with Denise George), released Feb. 1, 2011. Denise studied journalism at Harvard University and holds a master's of divinity equivalent from studies at Southern Seminary, Ruschlikon Theological Seminary, and Beeson Divinity School. Denise is married to Dr. Timothy George, founding dean of Beeson Divinity School, Samford University. She is mother to two children, Christian and Alyce. Her hobbies include spending time in solitude, spending time with friends, reading, writing, traveling, and fishing. You may contact Denise George at cdwg@aol.com or visit her website at www.authordenisegeorge.com.

http://encouragementforwoundedwomen.blogspot.com

Denise George

Also by Denise George

All these books, in hard copy, paperback, and as ebooks, can be ordered and/or downloaded through amazon.com, as well as other outlets. Some of these books can be ordered directly from the website: www.authordenisegeorge.com

NEW: *Learning to Trust Your Heavenly Father (Even If You Can't/Couldn't Trust Your Human Father).* From the *Come With Me to the Quiet Place* Series, by Denise George.

Daughters need kind, loving, and responsible dads in order to grow up emotionally, mentally, and spiritually whole. A human father most often paints for his daughter the portrait of her Heavenly Father. If her human father is/was trustworthy, she also views her Heavenly Father as trustworthy. But, unfortunately, the opposite is also true. *Learning to Trust Your Heavenly Father* will bring understanding, hope, and spiritual refreshment to women who have/had distant, absent, abusive, and/or undesirable dads.

NEW: *Learning to Pray When Your Heart is Breaking (Discerning and Discarding the Myths That Keep You from Forgiving)* Sometimes life can deeply hurt us. Learning to Pray When Your Heart Is Breaking tackles those hard questions of faith we may ask when pain turns our lives upside down. Questions like, Father, do you hear me when I pray? Do you have the power to answer my prayers? Do you love me enough to answer my prayers? Am I praying hard enough? How should I pray when my need is urgent? ...

NEW: Learning to Forgive Those Who Hurt You (Discerning and Discarding the Myths That Keep Your from Forgiving) Forgiving those who have purposely hurt you, and/or hurt someone you love, brings healing to your heart. Weeds of unforgiveness, if allowed to grow, can choke your spirit, make you bitter, and ruin your relationships and life. Learning To Forgive Those Who Hurt You will teach you the meaning of genuine forgiveness, and will show you how to discern and discard the myths that can keep you from forgiving others.

NEW: *I Am My Sister's Keeper: Reaching Out to Wounded Women*
We live in a world of hurting women. And just as Jesus compassionately loved those who were suffering, so can we. This book tenderly addresses issues like broken relationships and divorce; un-forgiveness; loneliness; spouse abuse; and loss and grief. Makes an ideal resource for groups of women to study together. Published by *Christian Focus Publisher*s.

NEW: *Fighting Fear With Faith: Weathering the Storm with God's Promises*
For many women in difficult situations, fear takes a powerful hold. The reasons, whether real or imagined, abound. Some fears are health-gifts from God to protect us. Many fears, though, are pretenders—tools of the enemy to harm us. This book helps readers to discern the difference, to remember God's promises and to appropriate God's great power. Ideal for individual or group study. Published by *Christian Focus Publishers*.

NEW: *While the World Watched: A Birmingham Bombing Survivor Comes of Age During the Civil Rights Movement* by Carolyn Maull McKinstry with Denise George

On September 15, 1963, a Klan-planted bomb went off in the 16th Street Baptist Church in Birmingham, Alabama. Fourteen-year-old Carolyn Maull was just a few feet away when the bomb exploded, killing four of her friends in the girl's rest room she had just exited. This book is a poignant and gripping eyewitness account of life in the Jim Crow South, and a uniquely moving exploration of how racial relations have evolved over the past 5 decades…and how far we have yet to go. Published by *Tyndale House Publishers*.

The Secret Holocaust Diaries: The Untold Story of Nonna Bannister by Nonna Bannister, with Carolyn Tomlin and Denise George

Nonna Bannister carried a secret almost to her Tennessee grave: the diaries she had kept as a young girl experiencing the horrors of the Holocaust. This book reveals that story. Nonna's childhood writings, revisited in her late adulthood, tell the remarkable tale of how a Russian girl from a family that had known wealth and privilege, then exposed to German labor camps, learned the value of human life and the importance of forgiveness. This story of loss, of love, and of forgiveness is one you will not forget. Published by *Tyndale House Publishers*.

Johnny Cornflakes: A Story About Loving the Unloved Based on the author's true-life story, Denise George learns that God works in unexpected ways and through unlikely people. This is a beautiful story that can be shared together as a family. Published by *Christian Focus Publishers*.

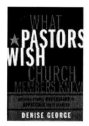

What Pastors Wish Church Members Knew: Helping People Understand and Appreciate Their Leaders
"A crisis is happening in the pulpits of our churches today. Our pastors are hurting in silence. They are suffering from physical exhaustion, overwhelming stress, painful loneliness, deep emotional scars, spiritual burnout, and disillusionment. They have a lack of money, lack of friends, lack of time, and lack of confidence in their abilities and ministries. Our pastors are leaving us. They are abandoning their pulpits—disappointed, disgusted, and deeply wounded—by the thousands each year." The results of George's research through anonymous surveys with hundreds of church pastors from 40 different denominations, will surprise, and maybe even shock, today's church member. Published by *Zondervan*.

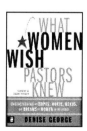

What Women Wish Pastors Knew: Understanding the Hopes, Hurts, Needs, and Dreams of Women in the Church "What do you wish your pastor knew about women in the church?" The question went out to hundreds of Christian women. This book is the result of that survey: powerful new insights and guidance that can help pastors build up women, heal them, empower them, and help them contribute fully and gladly to the church. This book will open your eyes to the needs, frustrations, dreams, and potential of your church's greatest resource—the 60 percent of its members who provide far more than 60 percent of what keeps it going. Published by *Zondervan*.

God's Gentle Whisper: Developing a Responsive Heart to God
This book challenges Christians today to seek an intimate dynamic relationship with God through three aspects of waiting on him in prayer: We know him by listening with our heart. We love him by hearing his voice. We serve him by responding to his gentle whisper. Published by *Christian Focus Publishers*.

Teach Your Children to Pray
A practical, hands-on tool for parents to use to help teach their children to pray. This book shows parents how to make prayer with young children creative, fulfilling, and fun! Filled with wonderful activities and ideas for today's parents and children. Published by *Christian Focus Publishers*.

Our Dear Child: Letters to Your Baby on the Way
Take heart from these encouraging letters written by Denise George and Timothy George to their son, Christian, before he was born. They are honest, heart-warming, and full of wisdom. This book makes an ideal gift for new (and "to be") parents/grandparents. Published by *Christian Focus Publishers*.

Check out www.authordenisegeorge.com to learn of new books by Denise George.

Endnotes :

1. I am using *spirit* as a synonym for *soul*. The two terms are interchangeable in the context of this book.
2. Thomas a Kempis. Quoted in Richard J. Foster and Emilie Griffin, *Spiritual Classics* (San Francisco: HarperSanFrancisco, 2000), p. 149.
3. Ibid, p. 150.
4. Ibid, p. 151.
5. Quoted in Philip Yancey, *What's So Amazing About Grace?* (Grand Rapids, MI: Zondervan, 1997), p. 270.
6. Quoted in Charles Swindoll, *Simple Faith* (Dallas: Word Publishing, 1991), p. 163.
7. Scott Savage, *A Plain Life* (New York: Ballantine Books, 2000), p. 150.
8. "Cruel and Unusual Punishment" editorial, *Cincinnati Post*, 8 March 2002. Quoted from Chuck Colson's *BreakPoint*, Commentary #020419 (19 April 2002), "Cruel and Unusual?"
9. Scott Savage, *A Plain Life* (New York: Ballantine Books, 2000), p. 95.
10. Ibid, p. 120.
11. Charles Swindoll, *Simple Faith* (Dallas: Word Publishing, 1991), p. 222.
12. John Updike, quoted in Philip Yancy, *The Bible Jesus Read* (Grand Rapids, MI: Zondervan, 1999), p. 27.
13. Allen Bloom, *The Closing of the American Mind*, quoted in Larry Burkett, *Women Leaving the Workplace* (Chicago, IL: Moody Press, 1995), p. 169.
14. Ibid, p. 168. "Adverse Health Effects of Noise," information from: www.who.int/environmentalinformation/Noise/Comnoise-3.pdf www.macalester, edu/psych/whathap/UBNRP/Audition/site/noiseeffects.html ;

www.city.toronto.on.ca/health/hphe/pdf/noiserptattachment-march 23.pdf
15. Ibid.
16. Catherine Marshall, *Adventures in Prayer* (Grand Rapids, MI: Baker/Chosen Books, 1975), p. 65.
17. Joseph Cardinal Bernardin, *The Journey to Peace* (New York: Doubleday. 2001), p. 33.
18. Quoted in John O'Neil, "Performance: A Quick Power Nap's Benefits," *New York Times* online (28 May 2002).
19. Paul Brand and Philip Yancey, *In His Image* (Grand Rapids, MI: Zondervan, 1984), p. 129.
20. Roger Sperry, quoted in ibid, p. 128-29.
21. Eric Chaisson, *The Life Era* (New York: W.W. Norton, 1989), p. 253-54, quoted in William V. Pietsch, *The Serenity Prayer Book* (San Francisco: HarperSanFrancisco, 1990), pp. 99-100.
22. Brand and Yancey, *In His Image*, pp. 132-33.
23. Henri J. M. Nouwen, *Making All Things New* (New York: Phoenix Press, Walker and Company, 1981), p. 72.
24. Karl Rahner, quoted in Richard J. Foster and Emilie Griffin, *Spiritual Classics* (SanFrancisco: HarperSanFrancisco, 2000), p. 219.
25. Ibid.
26. Diane Passno, *Feminism: Mystique or Mistake?* (Wheaton, IL: Tyndale House, 2000), p. 170.
27. Henri J. M. Nouwen, *Can You Drink the Cup?* (South Bend, IN: Ave Maria Press, 1996), p. 100.
28. Quoted by Richard J. Foster and Emilie Griffin, *Spiritual Classics* (San Francisco: HarperSanFrancisco, 2000), p. 160.
29. Wayne E. Oates, *Managing Your Stress* (Indianapolis: Bierce Associates, Inc., 1983), p. 3.
30. Anne Morrow Lindbergh, *The Gift From the Sea* (New York: Vintage Books, 1965), p. 96.
31. Susan Zarrow, "Stress: The Facts," *Prevention* magazine, Sept. 1987, p. 86.

32. Quoted from www.stress.org/problem.htm, "America's #1 Health Problem," from the *American Institute of Stress*, 124 Park Avenue, Yonkers, NY 10703.
33. Ibid.
34. Paul Brand and Philip Yancey, *In His Image* (Grand Rapids, MI: Zondervan, 1984), p. 255.
35. Zarrow, "Stress: The Facts," *Prevention*, p. 86.
36. Norma Peterson, "Daily Hassles Are Hazardous," *Reader's Digest*, April 1987, p. 76.
37. Quoted from: *Science Daily*, "Gender Doesn't Play a Role in Risk of Death from Heart Attack, Study," Science Daily, Feb. 22, 2011. Found at: http://www.sciencedaily.com/releases/2011/02/110222151342.htmAccessed: Oct. 31, 2011.
38. Colette Bouchez, "Women and Heart Disease: Key Facts You Need to Know," *WebMD*, Heart Disease Health Center. Found at: http://www.webmd.com/heart-disease/features/women-and-heart-disease-key-facts-you-need-to-know. Accessed: Oct. 31, 2011.
39. George Barna and Mark Hatch, *Boiling Point* (Ventura, CA: Regal, 2000), quote taken from the book from Barna's online Web page.
40. Ibid.
41. Arthur Gish, *Beyond the Rat Race* (Scottsdale, PA: Herald Press, 1973), p. 20.
42. John Ortberg, *The Life You've Always Wanted* (Grand Rapids, MI: Zondervan, 1997), p. 85.
43. 'Rescue Me, Elmo" from Crime Blotter, ABCNEWS.COM, compiled by Oliver Libaw, Sept. 5, 2001, online.
44. Thaddeus Barnum, *Where Is God in Suffering and Tragedy?* (DeBary, FL: Longwood Communications, 1997), p. 13.
45. Quoted from John Ortberg, *The Life You've Always Wanted*, pp. 83-84.

46. Lewis B. Smedes, *Shame and Grace* (New York: HarperCollins, 1993), p. 39.
47. Serena Gordon, *HealthScoutNews*, Feb. 11, online.
48. Caleb Stegall, "Open Saint Exupery's Box," *Touchstone* (March 2002), p. 18.
49. Dallas Willard, *The Divine Conspiracy* (San Francisco: HarperSanFrancisco, 1998), p. 206.
50. Joseph F. Girzone, *Never Alone* (New York: Doubleday, 1994), p. 98.
51. John Michael Talbot with Steve Rabey, *The Lessons of St. Francis* (New York: Penguin Group, 1997), p. 1.
52. Vernard Eller, *The Simple Life* (Grand Rapids, MI: William B. Eerdmans Publishing Co., 1973), p. 122.
53. Guy de Maupassant, *Short Stories of de Maupassant* (Garden City, NY: International Collectors Library, n.d.), pp. 9-16.
54. Richard J. Foster, *Prayer: Finding the Heart's True Home* (San Francisco: HarperSanFrancisco, 1992), p. 63.
55. Eller, *The Simple Life*, p. 114.
56. Henry David Thoreau, *Walden and Other Writings* (New York: Bantam Books, 1989) [first printing 1954], p. 172.
57. Albert L. Meiburg, *Sound Body, Sound Mind* (Philadelphia: The Westminster Press, 1984), p. 66.
58. Henry David Thoreau, *Walden and Other Writings* (New York: Bantam Books, 1989) [first printing 1954], p. 172.
59. Ibid, p. 174.
60. Thomas Szasz, *The Second Sin,* quoted in Doris Grumbach, *Fifty Days of Solitude* (Rockland, MA: Wheeler Publishing, Inc., 1994), p. 15.
61. Wayne E. Oates, *Managing Your Stress* (Indianapolis: Bierce Associates, In., 1983), p. 62.
62. David Hansen, *A Little Handbook on Having a Soul* (Downers Grove, IL: InterVarsity Press, 1997), pp. 46-48.

63. Matthew Henry, *Matthew Henry's Commentary* on Matthew 11:28, from *Christianity Today* online.
64. Joseph Cardinal Bernardin, *The Journey to Peace* (New York: Doubleday, 2001), p. 63.
65. Don M. Aycock, *Be Still and Know* (Nashville: Broadman & Holman 1999) p. 66-67.
66. Forrest Carter, *The Education of Little Tree* (Albuquerque, NM: University of New Mexico Press, 25th anniversary edition, Sept. 2001), selected pages through the book.
67. Brother Lawrence, *The Practice of the Presence of God* (Springdale, PA: Whitaker House, 1982), from the cover.
68. Ibid, p. 33.
69. Ibid, p. 46.
70. W. A. Criswell, *Why I Preach That the Bible Is Literally True*, reprinted in *The Library of Baptist Classics*, Timothy and Denise George, eds. (Nashville: Broadman & Holman, 1995), summary from selected pages throughout book.
71. Mother Teresa, *In the Heart of the World* (Novato, CA: New World Library, 1997), p. 20.
72. John Michael Talbot with Steve Rabey, *The Lessons of St. Francis* (New York: Penguin Group, 1997), p. 59.
73. Thomas Merton, *New Seeds of Contemplation* (New York: New Directions 1961), pp. 82-83.
74. Dallas Willard, *The Divine Conspiracy* (San Francisco: HarperSanFrancisco, 1998), p. 357.
75. Ibid.
76. Mother Teresa, *In the Heart of the World* (Novato, CA: New World Library, 1997), p. 19.
77. Frederica Mathewes-Green "A Daily Repentance Workout," *Christianity Today* online, Feb. 4, 2002.
78. Normajean Hinders, *Seasons of a Woman's Life* (Nashville: Broadman & Holman, 1994), p. 26.
79. Henri J. M. Nouwen, *The Wounded Healer* (New York: Image Books, 1972), p. 91.

80. Frederica Mathewes-Green, "A Daily Repentance Workout."
81. Charles Swindoll, *Simple Faith* (Dallas: Word, 1991), p. 128.
82. Leith Anderson, *Becoming Friends With God* (Minneapolis: Bethany House, 2001), pp. 246-247.
83. T. W. Hunt and Melana Hunt Monroe, *From Heaven's View* (Nashville: Broadman & Holman, 2002), p. 22.